HouseBeautiful

COLORS

FOR YOUR HOME

HouseBeautiful

COLORS

FOR YOUR HOME

The **ULTIMATE GUIDE**
to **CHOOSING PAINT**

HEARST
books

Contents

Introduction

Count yourself among the lucky ones! You've cracked the code to one of the most perplexing decisions a person can face: What color should I paint this room?

The beloved *House Beautiful* column called Paint (on which this book is based) continues to be the most dog-eared, torn-out, and photographed page in the magazine—decade in, decade out. And for good reason! These endorsements of specific paint colors are unadulterated, valuable, and sure to work because the advice is straight from the designer's mouth to you. Why ask a stylish friend for paint counsel when you can hear from a professional who has painted hundreds of rooms—beautiful rooms! So to the elite cadre of design talent that has shared these snippets of advice, these colorful little gold mines, thank you! These are shortcuts worth taking.

As you peruse this book, rest assured that when you fall in love, you can do so without reservation. Love the colors, imagine your rooms swathed in them, and then make it happen. To live in color is a gift worth sharing.

Sophie Donelson
Editor in Chief, *House Beautiful*

CHAPTER 1

Essentials
Tried-and-True
Favorites

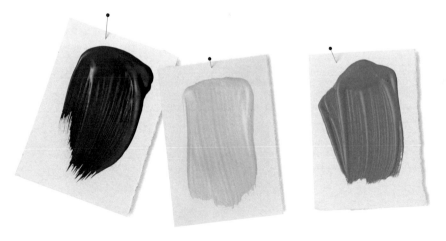

Timeless Colors

Classic hues always make the right impression.

"This classic hunter green feels like a color I've known my entire life—in the leaves of a magnolia tree, a sprig of fresh-cut basil, or my favorite flannel shirt in the second grade. In a Minnesota farmhouse kitchen, it has a comforting familiarity that evokes a sense of home. It's a color with soul, and that never goes out of style."

JEFF ANDREWS

**SHERWIN-WILLIAMS® |
SECRET GARDEN SW 6181**

"Use this if you have to paint a room quickly and don't know what to do. It's a home-run color—a dirty celadon that has been in the line forever. My mother, who was also a decorator, loved it. It works for any environment—modern or traditional, no problem—and with any color—blue, red, yellow, tangerine."
ATHALIE DERSE

PRATT & LAMBERT® | ANTIQUE WHITE 14-31

"If you swept this color up from the deep sea into your favorite room, you'd join the rest of the world, who have used it in Chinese porcelain, Dutch delftware, and Portuguese tiles. I spotted it in Lisbon's famous tile museum, and on the same trip, I saw a kitchen in Paris painted this color. Try it with glossy black trim and a pearl-gray ceiling."
WHITNEY STEWART

BENJAMIN MOORE® | CARIBBEAN AZURE 2059-20

"This steel gray, with a hint of blue, has a kind of strength and calm that feels very architectural, almost as if it were a material integral to the room rather than a paint color. When you're surrounded by it, the effect is like an updated version of a traditional paneled room—but a lot less expensive. I would do it in high gloss so it glistens."
STEVEN GAMBREL

PANTONE® UNIVERSE | MONUMENT 17-4405

"It's one of my all-time favorite colors, a warm gray that makes a room inviting yet still clean and crisp. It works with almost any scheme, but I like to use it with either gem tones or neutrals, such as creams, browns, and dark grays. I painted my own living room this color and after all this time I still love it, which means a lot!"
BLAIR HARRIS

FARROW & BALL® | SKIMMING STONE 241

"There's something heavenly about this pale blue. You see it in Renaissance paintings or an early-morning sky. It would look equally great in a contemporary setting with nubby Belgian linen, or in a more formal room with sparkling crystal sconces. Put a true white next to it and you'll see how wonderful and subtle it really is."
PAUL SHERRILL

PRATT & LAMBERT | WHITE SMOKE 26-2

"I tend to prefer more complex, layered tones, and this fits the bill. Lavender is the only color that's both warm and cool, and this particular shade is like quicksilver. It changes and evolves all day long. It's cheery in the morning, restful and calm in the afternoon, and sexy in the evening's low light."
OLIVER M. FURTH

DONALD KAUFMAN COLOR | DKC-36

"Red lipstick, red dresses, red walls—fabulous! Red makes you feel alive. It instills confidence. And there's another reason people really like to sit in red rooms—they're cozy. If you're afraid to do the whole thing, just start with one wall. Even one shot of red will have tremendous impact."

MARCY MASTERSON

FARROW & BALL | RECTORY RED 217

"This taupe is effortlessly chic. It reminds me of a warm stone color, something you'd see on the walls at the Louvre. Mixed with crisp Parisian black and ivory, it's truly a timeless combination. It would look especially stunning with gold or brass accents."

ERINN VALENCICH

VALSPAR® | CITY CHIC CI 51

"This is a rich, dramatic, yet relaxed dark chocolate that has a ton of depth. Many people are concerned about using dark colors on walls, but I find that they create such warmth in a room—somehow you feel enveloped in the best way."

ANNETTE ENGLISH

FARROW & BALL | MAHOGANY 36

"I'm not one for big pops of paint color, aside from the occasional bright front door. I prefer something more soothing, like this nice, true gray. Not too dark and not too light, it's classic, clean, and beautiful. It works with just about anything—green, blue, yellow—and would look great in any room of the house."

RYAN BROWN

SHERWIN-WILLIAMS | REPOSE GRAY SW 7015

Shift into Neutral

Misty lilac, midnight blue, soothing aqua . . .
New neutrals join the ranks of white, beige,
and gray—and the result couldn't be more
stunning.

"This is a good atmospheric blue that's as
light as air. It's completely enveloping but
doesn't overwhelm you, and that makes
it a great backdrop for art—or whatever
you want to put in front of it. Unlike
white, which is always in your face, this
sort of recedes. And that's what a good
neutral does. You want to know it's there,
but you don't necessarily want to know
why."

DAVID MITCHELL

FARROW & BALL | BORROWED LIGHT 235

"The warmth of this gray comes from the addition of a splash of beige. It's a greige that feels as comforting as a bowl of homemade chicken soup. I love using it in large open spaces, where your perception of the color changes as the light changes. Accent it with turquoise, scarlet, or tangerine."

PATRICK BAGLINO

BENJAMIN MOORE | REVERE PEWTER HC-172

"Drab colors are far more interesting when they're elusive, and this is one of those marvelous chameleon colors—it can read as gray, taupe, or green, depending on the light. I'd use it in a matte finish on walls, where it would be a great foil to warm whites, or in a high-gloss finish on trim. It's soothing, never murky."

ROBIN BELL

FARROW & BALL | STONY GROUND 211

"This mauvey taupe is as warm as a cable-knit cashmere sweater. You could use it all over a bedroom, not only on the walls but also on Roman shades, a duvet, and a throw. It would turn the room into a cocoon . . . very peaceful. Bring in ivory, gray, eggplant, or chocolate for contrast."

BRETT BELDOCK

SHERWIN-WILLIAMS | DOESKIN SW 6044

"Although typically considered feminine, lilac performs beautifully as a neutral when paired with strong, deep colors like charcoal, black, or navy. And this shade is the perfect balance of saturation and tone, like seeing a sunset through a soft filter. Try it in unexpected applications—the ceiling of a moody, masculine library; the interior of creamy cabinetry in a kitchen."

LAURA BURLESON

SHERWIN-WILLIAMS | WALLFLOWER SW 6281

"Years ago, a Fiorucci salesperson stared at my all-beige outfit and said, 'Well, beige is the rage.' I said yes! Beige is my dependable neutral that marries any white, even a white gone wrong. Best on walls in washable matte, this changes hues with the light, warms a chilly entry hall, and whispers 'Shhh' in the master suite. It's nearly foolproof."

JONATHAN TAYLOR

BENJAMIN MOORE | HUSH AF-95

"When people say they want a neutral, they're usually asking for something that steps back. This is a deep midnight blue, the color of the night sky. It's not provocative, it's evocative—referencing something deeper emotionally within ourselves. You feel as if you could float away in it. The dark color erases boundaries and makes this sitting room feel larger than it actually is."

RAY BOOTH

BENJAMIN MOORE | HALE NAVY HC-154

"This bold color is surprisingly neutral. It's the same earthy red that you see in pre-Columbian art, or an Etruscan mural, or a Turkish rug—it's universal. And it goes with anything. We used it in our front hall as a backdrop to a Chinese coromandel screen and a huge African wooden sculpture. It creates this incredibly warm, inviting entry that draws you into the rest of the house."

CAREY MALONEY

DONALD KAUFMAN COLOR | DKC-17

"My mother, the late Betty Sherrill, frequently quipped, 'I like all colors, as long as they are white.' But I think there's some truth in it. And then the problem always is, which white is the right white? This one lets the daylight be itself in a room and becomes golden at night, when lit with candles and—sigh—tungsten bulbs."

ANN PYNE

BENJAMIN MOORE | ELEPHANT TUSK OC-8

"This is the absolute perfect greige. No need to look any further. And it's amazing with a brighter contrasting trim. I love it so much that I've used it in three of my homes. In light-flooded rooms it feels cool and crisp. In darker, cozier rooms it's very soothing."

SHAWN HENDERSON

BENJAMIN MOORE | REVERE PEWTER HC-172

"People always think neutral means beige. Beige isn't a neutral. It's 'blah blah blah.' A good strong color can also be a neutral—just look at nature! You'll see forest green, sky blue, and this luscious brown, which also reminds me of a melting pot of chocolate. I have used it in foyers, dining rooms, and even in my own bedroom. For a crisp effect, paint the ceiling and trim a bright white."

GARY MCBOURNIE

BENJAMIN MOORE | BARISTA AF-175

"This saturated gray-brown-black is really an off-black—not that intense fortune-teller black but soft and sun-bleached, with depth and mystery. In a matte finish, it looks like a slightly smeared blackboard. It reads as black but it's not quite as hard, so it's easier to live with. And anything you put against it looks amazing."

PETER DUNHAM

BENJAMIN MOORE | GRAY 2121-10

"For a house in the country or by the sea, aqua is the new white. It's the perfect complement to greenery or an ocean view. The idea is for the wall color to be quiet so it can blend seamlessly with the outdoors. This blue-green is a pastel with personality. Keep the overall feeling serene with light floors, white trim, a touch of deeper aqua, and a few dark accents to anchor the room."

JONATHAN ROSEN

FARROW & BALL | PALE POWDER 204

"I surprised myself by painting my living room pink. But it's a manly pink, very warm and earthy. It must have some burnt umber in it to tone it down. Maybe I'm drawn to its architectural character, reminiscent of old walls in Venice or the color of bricks made from the clay in my native Tidewater Virginia. And it's an excellent foil for my deep green linen-velvet sofa."
RALPH HARVARD

FARROW & BALL | RED EARTH 64

"This is the palest of yellows, the perfect color for a room that doesn't get enough natural light. It gives you the impression of sunlight without being overwhelming. I used it in my guest room to give my friends a boost of energy and morning bliss."
VICENTE WOLF

PPG PITTSBURGH PAINTS® | LOTUS FLOWER 1206-1

"I fall in love with two or three grays every year. This one is very pure—it doesn't go blue or green or purple. I like gray because it has the ability to disappear and let you focus on what's in front of it. Some people say that about white, but for me, white is too bright. Gray is soft. It fills a space and makes it feel comfortable."
LAURA BOHN

SHERWIN-WILLIAMS | SENSIBLE HUE SW 6198

"I have a typical cedar-shake house in Southampton, and I painted the whole interior white. I wanted it to feel fresh. The doors to the patio are always open in the spring and summer, so it has a very indoor-outdoor quality. Visitors—like a neighborhood dog and little birds—feel free to come in and out."

MARY FOLEY

BENJAMIN MOORE | SUPER WHITE PM-1

"I love this particular blue for its cool freshness and versatile complexity. It's right on the cusp between blue and green, with just a touch of gray to add elegance. I used it for the screened porch in my cottage, where it's a respite from the heat of the summer sun. It would make any room feel light and airy."

JEFFREY DOUGLAS

BENJAMIN MOORE | PALLADIAN BLUE HC-144

"A hallway where I hang black-and-white family photographs is painted this teal green, the kind of 18th-century green you might see in a Robert Adam house in England. Look at it another way and it feels contemporary, almost Caribbean. In any event, it's so bright and cheery that it catches your attention and makes you want to linger to look at the pictures."

CHRISTOPHER MAYA

FARROW & BALL | ARSENIC 214

"Anything that brings more light into the house—pale paint, chalky-white furniture, sparkling crystal—is embraced. This is the quintessential pale blue—very light and ethereal, as if you're floating in a cloud. A high concentration of mineral pigments reflects more light, so the blue feels layered and translucent, as if it's not a solid color at all."

RHONDA ELEISH

FARROW & BALL | PAVILION BLUE 252

"Whenever I want to compress a space and make it warmer, I go to a darker color. This brown has a tinge of gray, which brings in some light and gives it a sense of plushness. In my butler's pantry, I paired it with Calacatta Gold marble to create a strong contrast. That gives me the look of an old Dutch painting, which also draws attention away from the imperfect architecture."

SUSAN FERRIER

SHERWIN-WILLIAMS | BLACK FOX SW 7020

"I wanted something different in my living room that would set off my brown sofa. And I have two small children who like to play there, so I wanted it to be cheerful. Lavender happens to be both a color and a neutral, so it's bright and soothing. Mix it with gold, brown, or white to make it more formal. Add purple and blue to make it more fun!"

NATALIE KRAIEM

BENJAMIN MOORE | NOSEGAY 1401

"I'm a pushover for muted, serene colors, and this gray-brown fits the bill, creating a warm, intimate entry. I like to use a darker color to begin with and then make the rooms radiating out from it lighter, to pull you forward. And I'll usually do the ceiling in the same color as the walls. Otherwise, it feels like too big of a disconnect."

THAD HAYES

BENJAMIN MOORE | BERKSHIRE BEIGE AC-2

"This is a powdery blue with some earth in it, and that warms up the color. I love the combination of blue and brown. It's calming. I'd even use it in a living room, with mahogany furniture and natural linen. And then I'd go all the way to black somewhere and all the way to white—it doesn't have to be in large quantities—so you have the full spectrum."
WILLIAM CUMMINGS

FARROW & BALL | SKYLIGHT 205

"This is a color you can't pin down—kind of a smoky white alabaster, with more depth than a traditional white, gray, or beige. But it still has the subtle neutrality. It would make a traditional space feel lighter and more contemporary. Bring in the bright jewel tones."
JOHN LOECKE

FARROW & BALL | BLACKENED 2011

"People walk into this living room and go straight to the window and the view of Long Island Sound. I wanted to bring the outside in, and this is a very natural color. Put a strong, saturated color like tangerine next to it for an unforgettable combination."
EILEEN KATHRYN BOYD

SHERWIN-WILLIAMS | SLEEPY BLUE SW 6225

Best Whites

The perfect white can be hard to find—
but far from bland when you do.

"One trend I'm seeing is lacquered
cabinets. For that, Super White is the
only white I know that doesn't have a lot
of blue in it. My other favorite is China
White, which has a smidgen of gray and
also lacquers beautifully."
ERIC COHLER

BENJAMIN MOORE | SUPER WHITE 0C-152

"You cannot go wrong with any of Donald Kaufman's whites, but I'm married to this one. And pay attention to the lighting. You can ruin a white kitchen if you don't have the right light — Philips makes a Warm White LED lightbulb that's my go-to."

SARAH BLANK

DONALD KAUFMAN COLOR | DKC-67

"This white has depth to it, while still being warm and classic. With neutrals moving more into the gray and taupe families, and away from khaki and gold, this is the ideal white for a cool palette."

SARAH FISHBURNE

BEHR® | SILKY WHITE

"It's a subtle off-white with a touch of cream, yet not too yellow. The way a white looks has everything to do with the amount and type of natural light. This would warm up rooms with a cool northern exposure."

SUSAN SERRA

FARROW & BALL | WHITE TIE

"We love this color because it adds an element of history. It's more of an antique white — great for creating a vintage feel."

JULE ELLER

VALSPAR | SWISS COFFEE

"The one color that people consistently pick for moldings and windows is White Dove. It has the softness of alabaster, with a little gray and a little yellow. For long-term livability, what helps is that yellow cast. Put it up against other colors and you'll see how well it works. It's practically universal."

DOTY HORN

BENJAMIN MOORE | WHITE DOVE OC-17

"This color pairs perfectly with Sterling Grey matte lacquer. They're both subtle grays in a range I call 'almost white.' When paired together, they read as white but give the kitchen a softer sensibility."

MARK WILLIAMS

SHERWIN-WILLIAMS | BIG CHILL

"In 30-plus years of design, I've tried and discarded literally thousands of whites. I even attempted to mix my own, creating ever more exotic combos and driving my painters mad. Trust me: Nothing compares to this. I've never seen anything like it—well, maybe the color at the horizon right as dawn breaks over the Aegean. I've dubbed it Jeeves, after the fictional butler: ever present, always discreet."

BENJAMIN HUNTINGTON

SHERWIN-WILLIAMS | ALABASTER SW 7008

"I am historically prone to a neutral palette, and this white has been my go-to for years. It's dead center between warm and cool, and it works equally well in traditional or modern settings. And it's a chameleon, taking on subtle changes in shade over the course of the day."

DARRYL CARTER

BENJAMIN MOORE | HUNTINGTON WHITE DC-02

"While I love color, I think no color can be the most elegant. If it's done right, it makes a strong and sophisticated statement without trying too hard. This shade was inspired by Deeda Blair's Georgetown living room, painted a rich cream that looked like cashmere on the walls. It has a touch of yellow and gray—I remember her saying that everything needs a hint of gray."

MARY MCGEE

BENJAMIN MOORE | MARBLE WHITE OC-34

"This color is so pure and clean. It's the gentlest yellow, a milk white with a bit of straw in it. It would work equally well in a historical house or a contemporary setting. Throw in some raspberry or burnt orange to offset all that quietness and shake up the room."

CHRISTINE MARKATOS

PRATT & LAMBERT | MILK WHITE 15-32

"With this foolproof, dependable white, all of the decision-making is simplified. It won't read yellow or look blinding, and it's the sweet spot where elegance, restraint, and understatement intersect. My entire house is painted this color, and it's so calming. The walls don't compete with the art or the furnishings, and I de-stress as soon as I enter the door. What's better than that?"

KELIE GROSSO

SHERWIN-WILLIAMS | GREEK VILLA 7551

"So many whites and off-whites are lifeless. They're too bland, or too cream. That's why I was laser-focused on finding the ideal shade of ivory, something that wasn't basic and would glow from the inside. About 100 paint-test colors later, this was the winner. Nothing bests it for giving a room dimension. It's unlike anything else— a total game-changer."

VIVIAN MULLER

FARROW & BALL | POINTING 2003

"Royalty summered in the area of Portugal where I grew up, and the interiors of their palaces kick-started my love of jewel tones. But it was tough combining bold colors like malachite and turquoise until I found this neutral. It's a glowy, almost gray hue that can calm dramatic colors so they don't overwhelm. With it, I can push the limits and be as gutsy in my designs as I am in person."

ELSA SOYARS

BENJAMIN MOORE | GRAYTINT 1611

Pas de Deux

Sometimes two is better than one. Brought together in a single room or adjoining spaces, these pairs reach new heights.

"The real story in this Florida kitchen is the oversized window and the big sky. One day we were staring outside, trying to determine the perfect color, and there it was, right in our face. The blue was grayed a bit to soften the intensity, and the center panels are the palest shade in that line. Painting the frames of the cabinets a darker color and tying it into the trim can be an unexpected choice."
ANDREW HOWARD

BENJAMIN MOORE | GULL WING GRAY 2134-50
BENJAMIN MOORE | WICKHAM GRAY HC-171

"For the foyer walls of a children's boutique in New York, I chose a rich and moody hue; for the main space, I went with a pale, silvery blue. The contrast between the dark, dramatic entry and the light, airy shop creates a sense of depth and spatial separation. A children's shop houses so many colors throughout the year—from blush pink to bright green— and I find dark, midnight tones to be grounding."
NICOLE FULLER

FINE PAINTS OF EUROPE® | WC-86

FINE PAINTS OF EUROPE | WC-77

"These two are far from gray and white! Anew Gray is like lichen, changing with the light, while Alabaster reminds me of the beautiful stone for which it is named—pure and strong. Even though white and gray are thought of as cool colors, these have just enough taupe in them to make them feel warm. I used them together as the wall and trim color in a historic home in Chapel Hill, North Carolina, and they provided the perfect foundation in a space where art and fabrics play the leading roles."
LISA MENDE

SHERWIN-WILLIAMS | ANEW GRAY SW 7030

SHERWIN-WILLIAMS | ALABASTER SW 7008

"These greens remind me of finely chopped parsley and capers mixed with a bit of fresh lemon juice and drizzled over a salad. I used Misted Fern as an alternative to typical white cabinets in a narrow mudroom where lots of activity occurs. It's calming, and it deflects dirt and day-to-day wear. The adjacent family room was painted Stolen Moments, a whisper of a green. Together, these colors have a quiet energy that isn't bored, predictable, or pretentious."

SHAZALYNN CAVIN-WINFREY

BENJAMIN MOORE | MISTED FERN 482

BENJAMIN MOORE | STOLEN MOMENTS 477

"I've been craving crisp white spaces, but with one surprise—a black dining room, powder room, or study. Black and white is timeless and chic, evocative of Chanel and glamorous Hitchcock films. This particular white is subtle, not sharp. And when you go from white to this velvety black, the contrast hits you. Immediately you feel the drama of the space. It slows you down and creates a whole new atmosphere. Any color goes with it. Accents like an apple green chair or an orange lamp become even more vibrant."

ANNIE MAHONEY

BEHR | WHITE TRUFFLE 720C-1

BEHR | BLACK SUEDE S-H-790

"In Morocco, green is a symbol of prosperity and fertility–it's a happy color. I turned to this pale version for a showhouse in Palm Beach, where I created a Middle Eastern–inspired tented room with walls of this green covered in white trellis and door and window frames in black. I was very influenced by the lush foliage outside, and the black, almost like a rich soil, provided a punctuation mark in a really wonderful, elegant way."

CHRISTOPHER MAYA

BENJAMIN MOORE | PALE AVOCADO 2146-40

BENJAMIN MOORE | BLACK HC-190

◄

"We wanted to make this 1850s Maine farmhouse feel playful and fresh. The paneling in the entry foyer had been painted some somber historic color, so we used this juicy coral red to wake it up. I love how welcoming it is. Then we painted the stair treads and handrail an earthy gray-green. One of the greatest things about a two-tone palette is that it allows you to pick out the architectural details of a room and highlight them."

KARI MCCABE

FARROW & BALL | RED EARTH 64

FARROW & BALL | CARRIAGE GREEN 94

"The owners of a classic Victorian in San Francisco were willing to take a risk and change up the traditional pastel palette, so we went for a moody, classy dark blue on the exterior. I carried that hue inside for the trim and picked a light greenish blue for the walls. Pairing colors from the same family is a successful layering approach: You start with one rich hue, then level it down. Introducing a color outside the blue family could have been distracting."

LAUREN GEREMIA

FARROW & BALL | TERESA'S GREEN 236

FARROW & BALL | HAGUE BLUE 30

"I first discovered Tuscany Green while doing a library in Aspen—the clients had requested a saturated color. It's an amazing chameleon: In some lights, it looks like an earthy, rich brown, and in others, it's a dark green. A crisp white on the trim provides a nice counterbalance. I like to pair these colors with materials such as rattan and light wood; with heavier furnishings and textiles, the room gets dark very fast."

KERRY DELROSE

BENJAMIN MOORE | TUSCANY GREEN 2140-20

BENJAMIN MOORE | SUPER WHITE OC-152

"Enveloping this Manhattan space in a stormy ocean blue that progresses into a contemplative gray cocoons you, like twilight descending into stillness. The secret is an ombré technique: Stiffkey Blue starts on one side, and more drops of Plummett are added to the paint until it morphs into full-on gray by the other side. The colors are so all-encompassing—they continue onto the ceiling—and the effect is so total, your mind quiets within minutes. It's exactly what you need in New York City—or anywhere."

TINA RAMCHANDANI

FARROW & BALL | STIFFKEY BLUE 281

FARROW & BALL | PLUMMETT 272

"Perhaps no color combination is more popular in the history of interior design than blue and white. It has lasted through centuries, from Chinese export porcelain to Dutch delftware. And for good reason— it's very versatile, equally at home in the city or the country. Do deep blue walls with my favorite white for trim, Atrium White."

JEFF LINCOLN

BENJAMIN MOORE | OLD GLORY 811

BENJAMIN MOORE | ATRIUM WHITE PM-13

A

"Striped walls create intimacy in a large foyer and take your attention away from awkward bump-outs that interrupt the room. I pulled the two blues out of the damask on the sofa. They have the richness of 18th-century American paint colors and create that fantastic vibrancy you get with blue on blue."

CARL D'AQUINO

BENJAMIN MOORE | ATHENS BLUE 797

BENJAMIN MOORE | NOVA SCOTIA BLUE 796

"The combination of red and blue is essential boho chic. Red walls can infuse a study or dining room with sultry energy, and navy baseboards help to anchor the space. Be careful not to pick a red with too much blue, or you might start seeing purple!"
ROBERT BROWN

BENJAMIN MOORE | UMBRIA RED 1316

BENJAMIN MOORE | NEWBURYPORT BLUE HC-15

"Imagine an inky indigo dining room in full gloss, accented by matte lilac paint on the corner niches. The blue-based lilac harmonizes beautifully with the darker blue; it makes the perfect backdrop for a mahogany dining table and chairs with lime-green cushions."
KEVIN ISBELL

FARROW & BALL | DRAWING ROOM BLUE 253

FINE PAINTS OF EUROPE | OPHELIA VIOLET 7172

"A rich gray provides an elegant contrast to a vibrant, sunny yellow. It's an unexpected combination that's both sophisticated and lively. Use it alongside creamy neutral fabrics, natural elements like driftwood or quartz bowls, and metallics for a chic Hamptons living room."

AMY LAU

BENJAMIN MOORE | BANANA YELLOW 2022-40

BENJAMIN MOORE | STORMY MONDAY 2112-50

"Pink and chocolate brown is one of those charismatic color combinations that simultaneously telegraphs gravitas and joy, striking just the right balance of prettiness and brawn. I love a room painted with deep brown walls, a pale pink ceiling, and white trim."

YOUNG HUH

C2 PAINT | BELLE'S NOSE BD 50

C2 PAINT | GOAT'S MILK BD 1 2022-40

C2 PAINT | CATTAIL BD 48

"These grays are just the calmest thing in the world, and the green in them means they go with everything. I like painting a wall in two shades. The darker color grounds the room, and then the lighter runs right up to the ceiling and makes it feel higher. It creates this serene atmosphere."

LAURA BOHN

SHERWIN-WILLIAMS | ALOOF GRAY SW6197

SHERWIN-WILLIAMS | SENSIBLE HUE SW6198

"When you're working with green and red, you don't want it to look like Christmas. So pick tonalities that are timeless, like the olive green and blood red we used in this informal dining room. It's the color of fall foliage and autumn chrysanthemums. If you look in nature, you'll find all these odd, wonderful combinations."
ALESSANDRA BRANCA

FINE PAINTS OF EUROPE | E10-59

FINE PAINTS OF EUROPE | E25-05

"Pink is such a warm, soothing color, and it instantly brings out the best in skin tones. Add a dose of citrusy green for a gorgeous pairing of sweetness and zing. Against white millwork, this is a phenomenal palette—a great option for dressing rooms, baths, or any room in a summer home."
LORNA GROSS

SHERWIN-WILLIAMS | ALABASTER SW 7008

SHERWIN-WILLIAMS | INNOCENCE SW 6302

SHERWIN-WILLIAMS | LIME GRANITA SW 6715

Room by Room

Location, location, location . . . Create a knock-out room—and another and another—with hand-picked shades for every space.

"Like an invitation to a party, a foyer should pique your interest. So I want something that has tons of wow factor, and this tomato red with coral undertones feels exciting and also makes people look good. It gives you a warm, healthy glow. The mirrored wall doubles the drama and reflects the dark chocolate walls in the adjacent dining room."

TOBI FAIRLEY

**SHERWIN-WILLIAMS |
EMERALD RED TOMATO SW 6607**

The Entryway

"This powdery green doesn't shout. It's a great backdrop for creating quiet drama, a moody color that looks as if it has been there forever. It works its magic over time. I teamed it with earthy black terra-cotta tiles, shimmering pops of gilt and brass, and an ivory-white Rococo console for flourish and freshness."

KATIE LEEDE

FARROW & BALL | ESTATE EGGSHELL LICHEN 19

"I tend to choose paint colors based on what I see in nature, and this reminds me of a cloudy sky just before a rainstorm. It has gray and blue and green in it, and that creates a very soothing transition from the outdoors. You feel comfortable and at ease. Antique gold light fixtures and a marble-topped console would add glamour."

PATRICK J. BAGLINO, JR.

BENJAMIN MOORE | AURA KENTUCKY HAZE AC-16

"After being out all day, I want to walk into a clean, uncluttered space. It should be neutral and relaxing, and this is the perfect greige. With crisp white moldings and black doors, it looks very handsome. All the pressures of the day would just fall away."

GRANT K. GIBSON

FARROW & BALL | DEAD FLAT MOUSE'S BACK 40

"I like to go big and I like to go bold in this transitional space. You're there for just brief moments of the day, so why not take the opportunity to have fun? I'm very into black on the wall right now—sexy, powerful, and as bold as it gets. With a mirror, a brass pendant, and a Moroccan tile floor in coral and white? Yum."
GENEVIEVE GORDER

VALSPAR | SIGNATURE® TUXEDO TIE AR2104

"This is like walking into a bowl of cheer. Do the walls in a shiny finish— but first the surface has to be smooooth, as Bobby Short would say—and then put silver paper on the ceiling, with clear lacquer over it. The furniture would be black and white, on a black-and-white floor—marble or painted. It would be glamorous forever."
THOMAS BRITT

**BENJAMIN MOORE |
ADVANCE TROPICANA CABANA 2048-50**

"I always try to give a foyer a little excitement. After all, it's the opening act of the show. I like this color because it reminds me of Milk Duds! Hard to resist, just like a chocolate-colored, mouthwatering room."
ANTHONY BARATTA

PRATT & LAMBERT | ACCOLADE BLACK COFFEE 3-19

"The color of a foyer should be deep, like this red-purple that reminds me of the center of a peony. Then the rooms radiating off from it should be lighter in color, as if the apartment is opening up. But first you have this moment of darkness and mystery, where you can organize yourself before you walk into the spotlight."

ANN PYNE

BENJAMIN MOORE |
REGAL® SELECT GRAPE JUICE 2074-10

"This is a fleshy pink, which makes it more sophisticated and versatile. With the right lighting, it really glows, and that's such a warm and welcoming way to be introduced to someone's home. Pair it with some strong, slightly masculine pieces to add visual weight. An antiqued brass mirror and a dark wood console would do the trick."

MONA ROSS BERMAN

FARROW & BALL | ESTATE EMULSION PINK GROUND 202

"This lush coral makes you feel as if you're walking into a conch shell. It's happy and bright. You might not be able to live with this amount of color in a living room, but in a small, featureless entry with lots of doorways, a dramatic paint color is the best way to create a sense of place."

VICTORIA NEALE

BENJAMIN MOORE | REGAL SELECT OLD WORLD 2011-40

The Home Office

◄

"When I chose the color for my library, I needed something sophisticated since it's next to the living room. This blue-gray is quiet and dramatic at the same time, which is the definition of elegance. It's equally lovely in the morning light or in the evening, lit by the glow of a lamp. It would also look great on kitchen cabinets."

MOLLY ISAKSEN

PORTOLA PAINTS & GLAZES® | SEAL 086

"This celadon is a little more serious than a lot of light greens. It's got a touch of gray, which gives it some depth. That makes it more earthy and sort of quiet, which is ideal for a work space. You get color and warmth, but it's not too much of a commitment. And it goes with everything, so it's a great backdrop."

SALLY STEPONKUS

BENJAMIN MOORE | HANCOCK GREEN HC-117

"Everything about this vivacious aloe green says, 'Let's go forward!' Able to give a room instant vitality, it has slight gray undertones, which I've contrasted with mustard-yellow leather chairs and a walnut table. It's fantastic in an office or library, but it will urge you to be bold, so make sure the space can handle all your confidence!"

CORTNEY BISHOP
FARROW & BALL | CARD ROOM GREEN 79

"Using a soft, sophisticated taupey gray on the walls, trim, and bookcases is a great alternative to a dark, traditionally paneled room—and a fresher look. All the colors in this upstairs office are soothing, making it the perfect place to reflect or catch up on work at the vintage campaign desk."

SUZANNE KASLER

GLIDDEN® | OLIVEWOOD 30YY 36/094

"Using a bright red for a home office can be a daring feat. But to me, the color personifies passion, energy, and creativity. I recently lacquered the walls of a home office/library in this powerful crimson and loved the result. It stimulates the senses to be especially imaginative."

BRUCE BIERMAN

BENJAMIN MOORE | HERITAGE RED PM-18

"An office at home is an escape. You go there to concentrate on work or reading. You don't need any distractions. For a client who wanted a clean, crisp, organized office, I chose a wall color inspired by the delicate blend of a local barista's café au lait. I feel very focused and productive when I'm sipping coffee."

EVE ROBINSON

BENJAMIN MOORE | WINDS BREATH 981

"This is not really blue and not really gray. It's kind of creamy-dreamy, like a beautiful cloud. I think of an office as a place where you just want to be calm and creative, and this is very calming—and very chic with a pop of navy or lavender. It's a blank canvas for whatever you're doing at the moment."

DAVID PHOENIX

FARROW & BALL | BLUE GRAY 91

"This wall was really asking for something. In the midst of a light, white room, the splash of chartreuse is very spicy and yet oddly neutral. It really sets off all the other colors around it, even the simple putty-white cabinets and the old sepia poster. It's a nice jolt of happy energy."

JACKIE TERRELL

BENJAMIN MOORE | EVE GREEN 2024-20

"The idea came to me after a surprisingly relaxing flight from Los Angeles to London. The lighting in the plane was programmed to sync with the duration of the flight, and it varied through a cycle of warm, tranquil colors—including this lavender. The flight crew told me the lavender was specifically chosen to relax the mind."

CHAD EISNER

PRATT & LAMBERT | HALF LIGHT 29-2

"Sometimes designing for a couple can make you feel like you're a referee at a battle of the sexes. This teal appeals to both men and women, which made it perfect for an office that was going to be shared. It's robust but not too bold, and it would infuse any space with understated warmth."

KERRY JOYCE

BENJAMIN MOORE | ST. LUCIA TEAL 683

"Lately, I've been having a good time with this deep gray. It changes a lot in different conditions. When the room is dark or in shadow, it seems almost black. But in direct sunlight, it's the color of a Baltic afternoon. So it's not boring. It also goes well with caramel leather chairs—something I can imagine putting into almost any office."

DAVID NETTO

FARROW & BALL | DOWN PIPE 26

"Burnt Caramel is something you never want in your kitchen, but paint it on the walls of your office and it will completely envelop you. Part vintage collegiate and part bold masculine, it's relaxing enough to make you feel as if you're in a lived-in library but happy enough to keep your eyes from dozing. It gives instant history and a bit of prestige, which I think every home office needs."

KYLE SCHUNEMAN

BENJAMIN MOORE | BURNT CARAMEL 2167-10

"I've always wanted to find the right project to use Off-Black. It reminds me of the color of the sky just before sunrise—a dusky black. I look to David Adjaye's Sunken House for inspiration: It shows how black can be used to emphasize another color, creating a beautiful balance. I'd use it strategically in an office space or in a bedroom. It has a calming effect."

DANI ARPS

FARROW & BALL | OFF-BLACK 57

"Working from home can be a real challenge. Just around the corner are all sorts of distractions, so a home office has to be both inviting and calm— a place where you can focus. I like this soft violet because it's barely there in the bright midday sun but gains richness as the light recedes over the course of the day."

MOLLY LUETKEMEYER

BENJAMIN MOORE | VIOLET DUSK 1409

"I used this delicate pink in my own home office, and I love it! It's feminine and flirty, but not too sweet because it leans slightly toward coral. Apparently pink has been shown to create calmness and peace of mind. Pair it with black and white for a counterpoint, or add deep emerald green to balance the softness of the pink."

TOBI FAIRLEY

SHERWIN-WILLIAMS | ANGELIC SW 6602

"I have a Windy City office, and trust me: Midwestern winters last forever. During the endless, bleak cold, you crave color, and that longing brought me to this fern green. A single wall in this hue was all that a pure-white kitchen in suburban Chicago needed to hint at warmer days to come. Also a plus: It brought out the cool tones in the silvery range hood and the gray upholstery of the stools."

FRANK PONTERIO

FINE PAINTS OF EUROPE | WILLOW BS12B17

The Kitchen

◄

"I couldn't not do an aqua kitchen for clients who love the ocean. Their home is in landlocked Arkansas, but they requested the relaxing, transporting blue-green of tropical seas, and this color nails it. The kitchen is open to the family room, and enveloping it completely in watery blues, from the island to the refrigerator panel to the tiled backsplash, helps it recede and disappear."
TOBI FAIRLEY

SHERWIN-WILLIAMS | TIDEWATER SW 6477

"In a large kitchen, I always do a contrasting color on the ceiling. It adds dimension and becomes a final, not-to-miss detail. This tan evokes sun-faded military bases out West. Partnered with black-mirror cabinets and counters and wenge-wood walls in a Miami home, it turned the kitchen into a sleek man cave. And it also complemented all the lush green fronds outside."
CHRISTOPHER COLEMAN

SHERWIN-WILLIAMS | CANVAS TAN SW 7531

"Talk about shipshape! My ideal cook space isn't a vanilla white—it's this jaunty, nautical navy blue. Rich and commanding, with cobalt undertones, it will transform any size kitchen into a gleaming jewel box, especially if you give it a lacquered finish. I see it with polished brass hardware and wide-plank wood floors."
CATHERINE BROWN PATERSON

FARROW & BALL | DRAWING ROOM BLUE 253

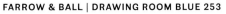

"There are so many ways to bring color into a kitchen, but my all-time favorite is as a surprise inside a cabinet. You open the door and—hello, gorgeous! I've done it in my own place, with this knock-your-socks-off orange. It's the exact shade of an Hermès gift box, so every time I go into one of the kitchen's fumed-oak cabinets, it's like unwrapping a happy little present."
PATRICK SUTTON

BENJAMIN MOORE | ELECTRIC ORANGE 2015-10

"I am so smitten with this color. It's right at the intersection of gray and green, that moment a stormy sky casts a shadow across a summer field. Both cozy and fresh, it's a little unexpected, and I treat it like a neutral in kitchens. It's sensational with brass hardware and plumbing, which is what I paired it with in a Deer Valley, Utah, chalet."
MELISSA WARNER ROTHBLUM

FARROW & BALL | GREEN SMOKE 47

"You've got to pack as much punch as possible into a tiny kitchen. For a Manhattan pied-à-terre, I knew this red would deliver. A glossy, glam scarlet, it recalls Mr Chow, the city's iconic Chinese restaurant, during disco's heyday. When I put this on an all-white kitchen's cabinet insets, drawer fronts, and moldings, it suddenly clicked with the rest of the apartment's Studio 54 vibe."
SASHA BIKOFF

FINE PAINTS OF EUROPE | TULIP RED 1001

▲

"For a breezy Palm Beach kitchen, I treated this wispy-cloud gray as an accent color. It's muted and calm, and on sunny days, it reads as the lightest, palest blue. Painting it on the cabinets and architectural details draws attention to the textures of the raffia wallpaper and pecky cypress ceiling while keeping the focus on the stunning limestone-topped island."

BETH MARTELL

BENJAMIN MOORE | PAPER WHITE 1590

The Bedroom

"I tend to like colors with a bit of gray in them. They're more sophisticated. This can look blue or gray or green depending on the time of day. It's got that Swedish thing—a tranquil, soft elegance. Beautiful with chalky-white wood and a bit of gilt. Red and aqua would also be divine."

ALEX PAPACHRISTIDIS

BENJAMIN MOORE | HEALING ALOE 1562

"This is a quiet green, like that pale green that you see in a hydrangea. It makes me think of summers in Nantucket. It would feel very serene in the soft light of a bedside lamp, as you unwind in the evening. Then when the sun comes up, it has enough color to give you some energy to start the day."

MARIKA MEYER

BENJAMIN MOORE | THORNTON SAGE 464

"I like real colors, as opposed to those that are just a hint of something. I love clarity, and this is a clear blue. Anything you put against it—a black bamboo bed, a bright abstract painting—will pop. And the light in the room takes on a wonderful atmospheric quality. You feel good in it."

HARRY HEISSMANN

VALSPAR | LYNDHURST CELESTIAL BLUE 5003-9C

It's hot here in Atlanta, and this gray-brown-green is peaceful and cool. I used it in my own bedroom with a four-poster bed dressed in white embroidered linen and a collection of creamware chargers hung on the walls. I love cream, white, gilt, and silver, and all those things look so pretty against this color."

JACKYE LANHAM

GLIDDEN | KHAKI GREEN 60YY 33/130

"Even if you're nowhere near the sea, this color makes you feel as if you're being lulled to sleep by the waves. It's not blue, not green, but somewhere in between. You will sleep soundly and wake up refreshed."

SUSAN ZISES GREEN

FARROW & BALL | BALLROOM BLUE 24

"Blue is light and airy, and this pale blue with bright white undertones sets off antique pieces in a way that makes them feel fresh again. It looks fabulous with any color. I love it paired with vibrant oranges and fiery reds. The effect is classic yet exotic—like an Hermès scarf. And who could resist that?"

JENNIFER BEEK

BENJAMIN MOORE | BLUE BONNET 2050-70

"I always consider the time of day that the occupant will be in a room, and in this case, the client was an early riser. This lavender feels good with the clear morning light. It has a drop of gray, which muddies it a bit and makes it more appealing to both sexes. Just don't use peachy or overly floral things. That's what takes it to granny town."

TIM CLARKE

PRATT & LAMBERT | QUARTZ MOON 31-29

"From the moment I open my eyes to the moment I shut them, my mind is going 100 miles an hour. So I want simplicity in my bedroom, not stimulation. This taupe invokes calm, and the hint of gray adds longevity. I'd pull out all the tones that are inherent in the color— brown, cream, white, gray—and use them for the furnishings."

JILL GOLDBERG

FARROW & BALL | JOA'S WHITE 226

"A bedroom is your refuge, your private space. When I walk into a room painted this color, I instantly feel the stresses and hassles of my day fall away. It's easy to let go, relax, and drift into dreaming, enveloped by this green-blue-gray. It's like a calm, cloudless sky. And it changes with the light."

MICHELE ALLMAN

MARTIN SENOUR PAINTS® | BLEACHED PILING 1125-A

"In our bedroom in a little California beach house, I wanted to create a soft, cozy box for sleeping. I draped the walls in an amazing lavender linen and found this paint to match. With undertones of gray and pink— like lilacs that have been bleached by the sun—it immediately calms the soul. Completely dreamy."

JAMIE BUSH

DUNN-EDWARDS PAINTS® | VIOLET CRUSH DE5946

"I wouldn't normally think of using red for a bedroom, but this burnt red is so subtle and complex that you can't help but feel embraced by its warmth. There's an echo of Pompeii—but it also has a totally contemporary vibe that makes it right for today."
TIMOTHY CORRIGAN

BEHR | RODEO RED 200D-7

"I know, I know, you're thinking, No man wants to sleep in a pink bedroom. But there's nothing baby or bubblegum about this pink. You could say it's the ultimate aphrodisiac, because there's not a woman alive who wouldn't feel pretty surrounded by this color. That's incentive enough for any man to go along with it, don't you think?"
SHEA SOUCIE

FINE PAINTS OF EUROPE | CAMELLIA PINK

"This is the silvery-greeny gray of a leaf of lamb's ear. It's so delicate and so soft. I'm especially drawn to it because of those silver undertones, which make it a little dressy and more mercurial. Keep the rest of the room monochromatic, with just a splash of bright Chinese yellow or orange."
ELIZABETH DINKEL

BENJAMIN MOORE | ICED CUBE SILVER 2121-50

The Nursery

◄

"I chose this blue for my daughter's room because it's so rich and yet still so subtle. It reminds me of a clear spring day and lends a happy feeling to the space. Pair it with painted furniture, colorful art, and blue-and-white fabrics for a sophisticated touch."

CECE BARFIELD THOMPSON

FARROW & BALL | BORROWED LIGHT 235

"The challenge in any baby boy's room is to find a blue that is stylish and doesn't yell baby blue. Because this shade has a twinge of periwinkle, I knew it would grow well with my son. White furniture pops against the walls, making the room look clean and crisp. As the years pass, I'll introduce chocolate brown and natural oak accents to give the space a more masculine, grown-up feel."

ALLISON DAVIS

BEHR | MISTY MORN PPU12-10

"When I was designing our son's nursery, I wanted it to be both tranquil and cheerful, so I selected this bright white. With its subtle blue undertones, it plays off the California light so beautifully that no matter the weather outside, Teddy's room always feels upbeat and calm—a true reflection of his personality."

OHARA DAVIES-GAETANO

VALSPAR | ULTRA WHITE 7006-24

"This cappuccino-foam hue is the perfect shade of greige. Its neutral tones look absolutely wonderful in all types of light, be it day or night. I love pairing it with creamy ivories and cool blues. It's warm and glowy, making it a wonderful choice for a nursery."

ALYSSA KAPITO

BEHR | COCONUT ICE OR-W6

"A beautiful blend of blue and gray that approaches robin's egg but is chalkier and more elegant. It's soothing and deep and will remain relevant as the child grows. For a boy, bring in café au lait tones and pops of strong olive green. For a girl, ground the room with dove gray and lavender accents."

AMANDA NISBET

FARROW & BALL | PARMA GRAY 27

"Pink can be jarring and loud—it's hard for the color not to scream *pink*! But this muted shade, with flesh undertones, is feminine and timeless. When the golden afternoon light shines through the windows of my daughter's nursery, it becomes slightly more saturated, like blushing cheeks. I always thought I was too cool to paint Georgie's room pink, but three kids later, I did it, and I'm absolutely in love with this magical hue!"

STEPHANIE SABBE

BENJAMIN MOORE | FAIREST PINK 2092-70

"I never even think about gender-specific colors! For an any-kid nursery, try this vibrant and verdant mossy green. Teamed with gray, white, pink, or blue, it has sophistication that will endure as the child ages and begins to insert his or her taste into the room."

SUSANNA SALK

BENJAMIN MOORE | DRAGONWELL CSP-930

"Shouldn't every child's day begin with sunshine? I think of the light streaming through a window in the morning, the warmth of it, and how it has a way of enveloping and comforting you. This mellow yellow creates the same feeling. Alive and chameleon-like, it lends itself to a multitude of palettes."

CHARLOTTE MOSS

BENJAMIN MOORE | CORN SILK CC-218

"When I want to find my next handbag in a paint color, I know it's a good one! This earthy hue has as much beige in it as it does pink—it's delicate and neutral. Mix in camel, crisp white, and a pop of rich garnet or navy. A nursery doesn't need to feel overly juvenile. As with a good handbag investment, paint selections for the littlest clients should stand the test of time."

PALMER WEISS

PRATT & LAMBERT | SWEET MIST 3-30

"I adore apricot for a girl's nursery. It has the warmth of a classic pink but is fresher and more invigorating, with subtle orange hues. Start out by including bright pink and orange accents, then swap in whites and teals as your baby girl grows."

SARAH VAILE

FINE PAINTS OF EUROPE | E3-26

"For a soothing neutral that works for both girls and boys, I like this pale lavender gray. It's polished and posh, and it won't look like an infant's nursery as he or she ages. For a more masculine feel, pair this color with moody navy blues and dark grays; yellows and pinks will add a more feminine touch to the space."

CHRISTINA MURPHY PISA

BENJAMIN MOORE | LILY WHITE 2128-70

"Toys are colorful, so why should nurseries be any different? While vibrant and energetic, this aqua hue acts like a neutral. Combine it with a wide array of colors, from pinks and purples to greens and yellows."

PHILLIP THOMAS

DUNN-EDWARDS PAINTS | SPEARMINT DE5729

The Bath

➤

"You'd often see this teal along the Amalfi Coast in the 1940s and '50s. The elegant blue brought Italy to this Hamptons house, contrasting and complementing the pale carved-marble tub—a nod to ancient Roman thermal baths—and emphasizing the high ceiling. A worldly color, it could chat as easily about 19th-century poetry as vintage Italian motorcars."

ACHILLE SALVAGNI

FARROW & BALL | DIX BLUE 82

"My clients were the catalyst for this hue. It's not what I would instinctively gravitate toward in a bathroom, but they requested an uplifting pink for their master suite. The surprise is how flattering it is—the peachy undertones bathe your skin in a warm glow. What could be better in a room where you're naked most of the time?"

MARY JO FIORELLA

BENJAMIN MOORE | FRUIT SHAKE 2088-60

"This is the gentle, serene color of the fog that rolls in every evening here in San Francisco. It's not a true gray; it has a blue cast to it that I find very soothing. A classic with staying power, it's great for a vanity, which is how I used it."

COURTNEY HEATON

FARROW & BALL | SKYLIGHT 205

"Along with being undersized, lots of bathrooms lack natural light. I counter the dimness with this take on robin's-egg blue, which to me symbolizes rebirth. Its subtle gray notes make it contemporary and give it versatility. Teamed with penny tiles, it can swing retro, and in high gloss, it's nonstop drama."

DONNA MONDI

SHERWIN-WILLIAMS | HONEST BLUE SW 6520

"With this soulful navy, I created a luminescent powder room that's like stepping into Vincent van Gogh's *Starry Night*. I painted it on the wainscoting and trim in a high-gloss finish, and its shimmer plays off the wallpaper's iridescent blue stripes and the cobalt marble of the vanity. The room is moody and swirling with crazy patterns—but it works!"

KRISTIN PATON

BENJAMIN MOORE | DEEP ROYAL 2061-10

"In a powder room with a bold marble basin in bright emerald green, dark lapis, and rich chocolate brown, I did this lush purple everywhere—the walls, the ceiling, the trim, the door. I chose a totally flat matte, and it's like being swaddled in cozy cut velvet. At night, when the light is low, it morphs into the deepest, ripest currant."

CHAD EISNER

BENJAMIN MOORE | GALAXY 2117-20

"This quiet gray is a calm respite from the wild, rocky waterfront view outside. Hazy and wispy, it doesn't overpower the bath, but it has enough depth to hold its own. Painting it on the ceiling and walls above the tile line envelops the space, smoothing out the assorted roof lines and wall angles into a seamless whole."

WENDY LESTAGE HODGSON

BENJAMIN MOORE | STONINGTON GRAY HC-170

"As a teenager, I was sailing off the coast of Maine when a squall hit. The churning, wind-whipped ocean turned this exact shade—a blue so deep it verged on black. For a powder room, I used it in a lacquer finish and the effect was instantaneous: The walls seemed to dissolve, and the space expanded. Black shagreen tiles underfoot were the finishing touch."

ERIC COHLER

FINE PAINTS OF EUROPE | NAVY BLUE 1798

"Imagine rich soil primed for spring planting. There's a touch of purple in it, which gives it a sensuousness that elevates it above basic crayon brown. I think of it like a neutral black, but better: It has the same presence, minus the hard edges. Smashing in a bathroom with crisp white trim, it also plays well with golds and pinks."

VANI SAYEED

SHERWIN-WILLIAMS | SABLE SW 6083

"On my latest trip to Paris, I spied this cosmopolitan green on doors so lustrous, I could see my own reflection—hello, unintentional selfie! I'm dying to try it in a bathroom. I see it with white marble counters and floors, an unlacquered brass faucet, and monogrammed towels appliquéd in a contrasting green—maybe lime or acid. Très chic!"

TRACI ZELLER

SHERWIN-WILLIAMS | ESPALIER SW 6734

"I love calming, spa-like colors for bathrooms. This is tranquil and airy, and it echoes the sea and sky. It reminds me of standing in the Caribbean surf, looking down, and seeing my feet through the crystal-clear water. Very changeable, it will read green in some lights and blue in others. I'd pair it with beveled Carrara-marble subway tiles and chrome hardware."
NICOLE GIBBONS

FARROW & BALL | GREEN BLUE 84

"There's something mesmerizing about lichen growing on bark. It's mysterious, hinting at the dark secrets of the forest, but also organic and approachable. This green captures that push-pull intrigue. Drench the walls of a powder room in it, then do the floors, trim, and vanity in an ebonized stain. You'll be seduced."
TRICIA HUNTLEY

SHERWIN-WILLIAMS | BONSAI TINT SW 6436

▲

"Your visitors will wake up to sunshine each and every day with this color. Yellows tend to go green or brown, but this shade is clear and bright. Guest rooms are a retreat from the norm, so I'd take a leap of design faith and pair this hue with a lush upholstered bed and mismatched side tables."

ROBERT PASSAL

VALSPAR | SOFT DUCKLING 3001-2A

The Guest Room

"Is it gray? Is it brown? Is that a lavender undertone? Depending on the light of the moment, yes to all! The chameleon of neutrals, greige is a wonderful background for rich jewel tones, like magenta and deep teal, or more tonal creams. As a client recently said, even the name is inspiring! Only use this color if you want your guests to stay awhile."
ALLISON TICK

BENJAMIN MOORE | HIMALAYAN TREK 1542

"It was the San Francisco fog of legend that motivated me to paint a guest room this layered hue, thick with the nuance of film noir. It evokes a feeling of 1950s glamour and mystery while also making visitors feel comfortably at home. This grayish plum is cocooning yet vibrant— warm at night and cooler during the day."
ERIC COHLER

PRATT & LAMBERT | CONFIDENTIAL 29-17

"The name alone should conjure up thoughts of a hot summer day. It immediately makes you smile! The warm, soft shade is a really pretty color for a guest bedroom and goes nicely with accents in sand. And it's not just an uplifting hue, it's also a very flattering one: Everyone looks great in it!
LINDSEY CORAL HARPER

BENJAMIN MOORE | MELON POPSICLE 2016-50

"Using white paint in a tropical space for guests just feels right. With the blue sky and strong sun and lush vegetation, one should not compete with a strong color inside. Plus, white bedrooms are a thing of romance and magic. Drape a bed with a million miles of eyelet and make it up with crisply ironed sheets, and you have a dream."

AMANDA LINDROTH

FARROW & BALL | POINTING 2003

"Don't call this pink! This is the anti-pink. It's fresh, modern, and sophisticated. And while it suggests femininity, men love it too. This soothing blush makes us all look good when the light reflects against the walls and illuminates our skin. Pair it with silver accents and refreshing splashes of early spring green. Guests may want to take up permanent residence!"

EVE ROBINSON

BENJAMIN MOORE | OPAL OC-73

"Guest rooms are an opportunity to be a little wild with an unexpected color. You might not want to live with this spinach green every day, but in a spare room, the deep hue feels enveloping and promotes relaxation. And everything goes with it. I never second-guess a color found in the beauty of nature."

PHOEBE HOWARD

SHERWIN-WILLIAMS | RELENTLESS OLIVE SW 6425

"This velvety navy is so deep, it almost looks black. The darker tones make the corners of a space less pronounced, so even the smallest of guest rooms will appear infinitely larger. I love adding pops of kelly green and orange accessories to play up the warmth and richness of such a classic hue."

LANCE JACKSON

SHERWIN-WILLIAMS | DIGNITY BLUE SW 6804

"Orange can be tough. Too much yellow and it feels hard, but just that subtle peach tone makes it happy and playful. I painted our guest room this hue, and people have always loved it. It's warm and inviting, yet somehow also soothing."

LIBBY CAMERON

BENJAMIN MOORE | CALYPSO ORANGE 2015-30

"I find this to be one of the most sensual off-whites. Because it has a tiny bit of putty in it, this color looks wonderful with sumptuous taupes and grays as well as crisp, fresh whites. It makes for a peaceful space that is calm and comfortable—precisely how one would want a guest to feel during a long weekend away."

BETH WEBB

BENJAMIN MOORE | CHINA WHITE PM-20

"An ideal guest room welcomes you home and makes you feel as if you are the first and only person to stay there. This shade feels homey and clean at once. It's the perfect soft neutral. It feels fresh and light in the sun and cozy in the fog or rain."

ALLISON DEHN BLOOM

SYDNEY HARBOUR PAINTS | MANUKA

"Reminiscent of ocean waters and vacation skies, this serene blue creates an idyllic retreat. It has a hint of green and soft gray and pairs well with navy, lime, or white. If timeless beauty and Zenlike calm combined to produce a color, this would be it."

JENNIFER COLEMAN

BENJAMIN MOORE | BLUE HAZE 1667

"I love this sexy, smoky hue—it's like lying on a beach at night and looking up into the sky. It's an unlikely and intriguing neutral for a bedroom. But when paired with polished chrome, lacquered furniture, and a touch of Bordeaux, it will leave your guest wanting to stay a few extra nights."

LYTEL YOUNG

DUNN-EDWARDS PAINTS | CAVERNOUS DE6364

The Masculine Space

◄

"Forest green calls to mind hunting lodges, gentlemen's clubs, and smoky billiard rooms. The lower the lights, the darker and more sultry this color gets, until it's almost black. Then, when the sun hits, it brightens up quite a bit. It's a traditional color in a modern room—a calm, curated space where a man would want to hang out."

WILL WICK

C2 PAINT | CHARGREEN C2-694

"Rather than going for the immediate 'wow,' men tend to like something more modest and understated. And they appreciate the complexity of a color like this, which sometimes reads as blue and at other times green, depending on the light. I see it in a study, where I would pair it with an aged-leather chesterfield sofa and gold or silver accents, to liven it up."

BENNETT LEIFER

FARROW & BALL | CHAPPELL GREEN 83

"For men, navy blue paint is the equivalent of a navy blue blazer—classic and comfortable. And the deep, rich color completely envelops you. I'd do watermelon-red upholstery for an eye-catching contrast, or you could try camel, mulberry, or brown. It's very versatile."

HEATHER HILLIARD

FARROW & BALL | STIFFKEY BLUE 281

"This is a macho neutral—muddy, earthy. It makes me think about getting on a dirt bike or hanging out on a boat, in khaki shorts and docksiders. The client wanted cool in his dining room and he got it, with strong sculptural furniture, edgy art, and a Murano glass pendant. No rug, no fuss."

DARREN HENAULT

BENJAMIN MOORE | COCOA SAND 1122

"This saturated Roman red conveys the solidity of Mediterranean terra-cotta, with a sprinkling of cinnamon. It's earthy and masculine, offering a nice counterpoint to white plaster casts and other souvenirs of the Grand Tour that I'm imagining in the room. Collectors understand that color can do great things for art. I'd do the trim in off-black or cream."

PETER PENNOYER

FARROW & BALL | PICTURE GALLERY RED 42

"So many men want a room that feels comfortable, and I don't think that necessarily means leather and antlers. This is the color of a dark thoroughbred horse. Brown is handsome, solid, and never goes out of style. I used it in the library of our house in Kentucky and paired it with graphic fabrics and a cobalt blue David Hicks rug. I choose Hollandlac in Brilliant for a luscious lacquered look."

MATTHEW CARTER

FINE PAINTS OF EUROPE | E25-30

"The words *masculine* and *pink* don't usually collaborate, but the name of this color is deceptive. It's actually a bullish, ruddy tan that brought a cozy warmth to a gentleman's library I designed for a Los Angeles house. Furnished with deep, comfortable sofas in autumnal russets, ochers, and blues, it's nicely suited to a glass of brandy, an inviting book, and a good cigar."

THOMAS CALLAWAY

FARROW & BALL | ENTRANCE HALL PINK 61

"Few things say 'chic bachelor pad' as much as a dark, moody color on the walls. This deep charcoal with smoky bronze undertones is velvety, intense, and undeniably masculine. So sexy! It's like a little dose of testosterone in a paint can. No wonder my client is no longer single."

JEFF ANDREWS

PRATT & LAMBERT | ANUBIS 32-17

"I'm a big history buff, and George Washington used this in his dining room at Mount Vernon. It's a striking verdigris, more vivid than a classic Georgian green, and he thought it was 'grateful to the eye.' In candlelight, it has a beautiful, moody glow. I know because I used it in my own dining room. If it was good enough for George, it's good enough for me!"

FRANK DE BIASI

**FINE PAINTS OF EUROPE |
SMALL DINING ROOM GREEN MV3**

"I'll often paint interior doors and furniture a rich black. It adds a strong masculine component to a room that makes it feel timeless. I think men like black because they wear it all the time. It's familiar, so it feels safe. But it also reads as a bold choice."
GRANT K. GIBSON

FARROW & BALL | PITCH BLACK 256

"If I had to pick a name, I would call this Spanish Moss, which hangs from almost every tree here in New Orleans. It's a soothing gray-green that's very elegant, with a bit of oomph—but not too much. I've found that women are naturally open to exploring the possibilities of color. Men keep themselves in a tighter box. But every single time I've used this, the men love it."
HAL WILLIAMSON

BENJAMIN MOORE | NANTUCKET GRAY HC-111

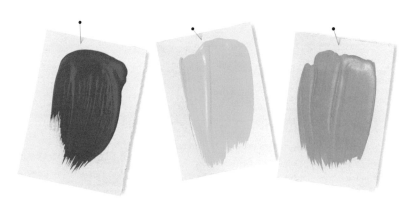

CHAPTER 2

Unexpected Shades

Colors with Personality and Point of View

Rethink Pink

Say goodbye to those bubble-gum sweet connotations. The versatility of pink continues to surprise.

"Imagine a sunset on an August evening, with the fading light shading the sky a gorgeous gray-tinged pink—that's this color. It's restrained and refined in this Manhattan living room, and it serves as a foil to the black sofa and patinated-bronze coffee table. This apartment is in a skyscraper that dates to 1929, so the pink is a nod to the luxury and exuberance of the Art Deco period. It also references the views of faded redbrick buildings outside."

JAMIE DRAKE

**BENJAMIN MOORE |
SALMON PEACH 2013-50**

"How joyful is this bougainvillea pink? It wouldn't be everyone's pick for a library in a very proper Washington, D.C., townhouse, but it was for one client. The owners were young, with toddlers, and it just made sense to have a little fun. You open the library door and—surprise! It's like the jolt of color you get cutting into a pomegranate. Cocoa browns help balance out the intensity."

ALESSANDRA BRANCA

BENJAMIN MOORE | ITALIANO ROSE 2087-30

"No argument here, this is a sweet pink. But I wouldn't describe it as confectionary. It's lighter and more delicate, like floating cherry blossoms. Of course, it would be sensational in a girl's bedroom. Team it with painted Gustavian furniture and one of those romantic metal chandeliers that look like a cascade of flower tendrils."

BENNETT LEIFER

BENJAMIN MOORE | PINK LACE 2081-60

"The beauty of this shell pink, which reminds me of my 1920s mother-of-pearl compact case, is its ephemeral quality. As the day progresses and the light changes, the color gains complexity. For an entryway or living room, I'd give it a high-sheen lacquer. What's more, this color is flattering to anyone in the room."

KELLY WEARSTLER

PRATT & LAMBERT | COY PINK 3-28

"This pale pink takes me back to childhood summers at the shore. It's the same color as the snack bar's strawberry ice cream that would dribble down my swimsuit. Those beach memories are probably why I once paired it with a fabric patterned with magenta seaweed for a little girl's room. The effect is like an undersea fairy tale."

ELIZABETH PYNE

FARROW & BALL | GREAT WHITE 2006

"In a sitting room with upholstered graffiti walls and bold botanical chairs, I couldn't not have this ceiling. This pink straddles classic and au courant, and it immediately upped the glamour in the room. We gave it depth and sheen with a glossy Venetian plaster, and it glows like a pearl. That bounces light around and makes the ceiling seem higher."

PHILIP THOMAS

BENJAMIN MOORE | PINK SWIRL 2171-70

"I adore pink! It's the color of romance, of plush bedrooms and posh dressing rooms. For a living room, I did this blush pink in a very monochromatic way, with upholstered pieces in the same hue. Accents of bright white and gold, touches of crystal, and a 1940s French bibliothèque put its mystique in motion. Pairing pink with handsome antiques brings out the color's quiet strength."

WINDSOR SMITH

BENJAMIN MOORE | WARM BLUSH 892

"At first glance, this lush pink almost looks too vibrant, but there are blue undertones to it. It's very much the color of India and of antique silk saris and jeweled bangles. I can see it as an accent wall in a white or soft gray room. Or you could drench a powder room with it, and it would be like celebrating Holi—the Indian festival of colors— every day!"

YOUNG HUH

BENJAMIN MOORE | PEONY 2079-30

"Let's call this my curveball color. Rich and saturated, it's alluring and fresh. I would add it to an understated room to deliver a pop of unexpected pizzazz. It would also be a knockout mixed with a flannel gray or wet-concrete gray— so chic and neoclassical."

MARTYN LAWRENCE BULLARD

BENJAMIN MOORE | CRUSHED VELVET 2076-10

"Combining pink with more soulful colors gives rooms a push-and-pull tension of opposites. I gravitated toward this shade when a client requested a pink dining room. It's pink, but more fleshy and taupey. After I painted the trim a contrasting red, the whole room fell into place. It was like pairing a dewy, rosy complexion with a scarlet lip—very ingenue meets leading lady."

TRICIA HUNTLEY

BENJAMIN MOORE | MILK SHAKE 1165

"I'm about to paint my office, and this is the color I chose. It's a gentle peachy pink that's crisp and cool, yet also warm. And it's exactly what you need when you're working: It wakes you up and keeps you alert, but it's peaceful enough that you can still concentrate. This pink will be amazing with glossy white bookshelves, linen curtains in a darker pink, and floral chintz pillows."

LINDSEY LANE

FINE PAINTS OF EUROPE | E3-1

"You know how beautiful a pearl necklace looks against skin? Maybe that's why this appeals to me. It's the softest, most luminous pearl with just the slightest hint of pink. Paired with silver hardware, cream trim, and Thassos marble, it would make the most elegant dressing room. Add slate or navy to intensify the effect with some contrast and drama."

JOAN CRAIG

VALSPAR | DANCE OF THE GODDESSES 23-1A

"You might think pink is only for a nursery or a bedroom, but this sophisticated pale pink would be stunning in a living or dining room. I like the fact that it's unexpected. It feels so and romantic, and it would be intriguing accented with strong colors like charcoal gray, black, orange, or red."

GINGER BREWTON

BENJAMIN MOORE | WARM BLUSH 892

"Warm tones are kind to everyone, but the pink family can be tricky. You don't want your room to end up looking like Barbie's Dreamhouse. This complex shade of coral hits all the right notes. It's chic, cozy, and incredibly flattering—perfect for this master bedroom."

SUZANNE TUCKER

BENJAMIN MOORE | CORAL GLOW 026

"Everyone knows that pink is flattering, and as a brunette with a perpetual suntan, I'm drawn to bold, saturated pinks. I used this color in a guest bedroom—after all, every host wants her guests to feel good about themselves—with grass greens, light pink–and–white fabrics, and a beige wall-to-wall carpet. When the wife walked in, she said, 'I wish this were our room.'"

ELIZABETH PYNE

SHERWIN-WILLIAMS | DRAGON FRUIT SW 6855

"While watching the Academy Awards, I was struck by how beautiful the starlets looked in pink. They simply glowed! What better color to surround yourself with in your bathroom? Simply fill the tub and feel pretty, calm, and soothed. No plastic surgery needed here . . . just a glass of pink Champagne! Cheers!"

MELANIE TURNER

FARROW & BALL | CALAMINE 230

Classic Bolds

With a powerful hue it's go big or go home. A trip to the far end of the spectrum can revive tricky spaces.

"My relationship with this decadent red began when I moved into a tiny, sunless tenement in Manhattan. I went full-on opium den in the living room and painted all of it this color—walls, trim, doors, even the pressed-tin ceiling! People thought I was nuts, but it taught me that it's OK to break the rules. Fast-forward to now, and this is still the glossy red I rely on for drama. Here, it cranks up the suave in a client's entry."

NICK OLSEN

FINE PAINTS OF EUROPE | TULIP RED 1001

"It seems everyone has been seduced by gray. Not me—I was a forever-steadfast fan of white. But my aha moment came when a client asked for a revamp of a wood-paneled library. I took a leap of faith, painted the walls this shade, and was shocked at how the gray cozied up the space, how it paired so well with camel hues, how it was both refined and chic. Consider me a convert!"

PAT HEALING

FINE PAINTS OF EUROPE | G22730

➤

"This egg-yolk yellow upended my life. Mesmerized by the color in this iconic 1950s photo of Nancy Lancaster's London drawing room, I was determined to join the design firm that she made famous. Lots of work-permit drama later, I moved to England—and my desk was in this very room! Up close, the yellow is bright and happy but also deeply sophisticated. I never grew tired of it, especially in the gray British light. It's a color lesson I remember whenever I want to bring warmth and punch to a space."

CATHERINE OLASKY

PORTOLA PAINTS & GLAZES | LOTUS PC195

"Thumbing through a book on Italian Renaissance paintings, I was awed by the rich blue robes worn by the Madonnas. In that instant, I knew: Deep teal speaks to my soul. It's pure and true, and it satisfies my longings to be comforted—but also to be swept up in the mysteries of life, of infinite starry skies and the dark, deep sea beyond the reef. Is it any wonder I've used it in every room imaginable?"

KATIE LEEDE

PRATT & LAMBERT | MIDSUMMER GALE 26-17

"I discovered this vibrant green in my garden before I spotted the paint chip. It brings the outside in and reminds me of how fun color can be. I've paired it with yellow, black, and white in my guest bedroom, and first-time visitors are always surprised by its vividness. I consider it my unsubtle way of persuading them not to fear color—a lifelong campaign of mine!"

SHEILA BRIDGES

BENJAMIN MOORE | BABY FERN 2029-20

"Let's paint the town red! What color could be better amid the bustling excitement of a metropolis? It's bold and up for anything, with the sexy energy of a suave cocktail party. I love it as an accent with neutrals and have painted it on ceilings, the backs of bookcases, and a niche behind a sofa. So striking in a lacquered finish."

GARROW KEDIGIAN

BENJAMIN MOORE | RAVISHING RED 2008-10

"Shining in a high gloss, this modern, exotic green utterly transforms the mood of a Fifth Avenue apartment. During the day, against the gray backdrop of stone and steel, it's like the silk lining of a bespoke suit. At night, as the skyscrapers glitter, it's as luminous as a moonlit ocean. The aliveness of the color is jaw-dropping."

PHILIP GORRIVAN

FINE PAINTS OF EUROPE | H03010

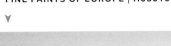

"Unapologetically glamorous, this vibrant teal with a Deco soul is the peak of chic. I imagine it's what a bon vivant world explorer would choose for his penthouse. In Uncle Harry's, a private club atop a San Francisco luxury high-rise, I teamed it with shiny black patent leather, velvets in tiger stripes, Moroccan rugs, and croc-stamped caramel leather. Glorious!"

KEN FULK

BENJAMIN MOORE | TROPICAL TURQUOISE 2052-30

"Like all the pinks I'm drawn to, this has some spice with the sugar. Those orangish undertones make the swatch look different—a little bit peach. It's not until you scale up the color to room size that you realize it's genius. Since it's more nuanced than sweeter, frostier pinks, you can combine it with shades that usually clash—oranges, reds—and pull off a room with amazing vibrancy."

ALLISON TICK

BENJAMIN MOORE | BERMUDA PINK 016

"Orange has a difficult reputation for a reason. To start with, you have to get the proper tone. This color has it, and in a room it reads as luxurious—it's reminiscent of an Hermès box. But then the lighting also has to be right; it needs to be warm, not blue. LED bulbs or incandescents are a must. Get the lighting correct, and this color will envelop you in warmth."

KELLY WEARSTLER

DUNN-EDWARDS PAINTS | ORANGE DAYLILY DE5145

"The moment I spotted this Black Forest green on the walls of a Los Angeles store, I was a goner. What struck me was the depth of the color, how it's timeless and current—both hip club decor, distressed to suggest the patina of age, and an actual centuries-old hunting club in Europe. A total departure from my staple palette of neutrals, it's opened an entirely new, intriguing world for me."

HEIDI BONESTEEL

PORTOLA PAINTS & GLAZES | HYDE PARK 107

"It evokes the 1940s, but this bleached terra-cotta—imagine a sunset reflecting off an adobe house in the desert—is due for a revisit. For me, it recalls an iconic Slim Keith photo from that era. She's lounging against pillows in this same shade of orangey pink, and while she's in repose, there's an energetic sophistication happening. It creates the same mood in a room."

FRANK DE BIASI

SHERWIN-WILLIAMS | SUNSET SW 6626

"The changeability of this chameleon gray, how it can take on the characteristics of the light around it, is very now. It's never the same, never static, always in flux—isn't that our wired world? In an elegant bedroom, I surrounded it with lavender and saw hints of the softest, most perfect lilac emerge."

BENNETT LEIFER

BENJAMIN MOORE | SHORELINE 1471

"Although this blue is about as scary as a Smurf, it frightened my clients. They felt it was too strong and intimidating for the mudroom of their Florida beach home. Fully committing to the color for the cabinets and the walls was the trick to changing their minds. The rest of the house is neutral, and this is an escape, like swimming in cool water. It's now their favorite room!"
MELANIE TURNER

RESTORATION HARDWARE® | DUSK

"At first glance, this blue is powdery and soft, almost like a pastel. Then you see it in situ, and you immediately understand its moody depths and complexity. You're struck by the richness, the mystery, and the timelessness. Because it both calms and intrigues, it's perfect for a bedroom. I love the way it interacts with wood tones, warmer neutrals, and antiques."
CALEB ANDERSON

BENJAMIN MOORE | VAN COURTLAND BLUE HC-145

"After I confidently suggested this intense blue for a client's study, I started second-guessing myself. What designer hasn't chosen a saturated blue only to find that it's more downbeat than moody? Thankfully, this sprang to life as it was applied to the walls—it's lively and oh so chic! I realized it's the exact blue of the gorgeous tiles I saw at the mosques all over Turkey."
RYAN SAGHIAN

SHERWIN-WILLIAMS | NAVAL SW 6244

"When people seek out dark colors they often pick blacks or grays, but there's a versatility to deep purple that I think would surprise them. To me it's a neutral, and its ability to create a layered, intimate room is almost magical. You can bring out its luxe side with gold tones, be bold and partner it with orange, or soften it with creams. Trust me: Try it in a dining room, and you'll be enamored."

ELENA FRAMPTON

BENJAMIN MOORE | SHADOW 2117-30

"Skip over this daring blue, and you'll miss one of the happiest, sunniest colors going. It's more playful than it lets on, and I find it works wonders in light-challenged rooms. I didn't realize its mood-boosting powers until I did a ground-floor dining room in Brooklyn with khaki walls. Adding this to the built-in cabinets made the space as uplifting and cheerful as a summer day."

SUZANNE MCGRATH

FARROW & BALL | INCHYRA BLUE 289

"I hesitated with this hue. It's historical and classic, a bit sentimental, and evocative of Wedgwood porcelain. So far, so good! Still, I worried it could skew somber. My plan was to use it in a music room, and while it was being painted, I anxiously held my breath: Would it drag down the energy in the space? Turns out, it's soulful. It simultaneously grounded and elevated the room."

LATHEM GORDON

SHERWIN-WILLIAMS | DEBONAIR SW 9139

▲

"This gray-black reminds me of shadows— for me, that's a good thing!—and I envisioned it on the walls, bookcases, and ceiling of my husband's study. But what I thought of as cozy, he worried would be oppressive. Ultimately, he loved it. With the gold overhead light and leather chair, it's tailored and masculine, not cave-like."

CARMEL GREER

CLARK+KENSINGTON® | BLACK CHIFFON N-C15

"Often the initial reaction to this olive green is that it's dark, maybe even a little dingy. It doesn't seem like it would get you rah-rah excited or inspired. But don't underestimate it! It has a sophistication that's ideal for millwork and trim, which I took advantage of in a library. Paired with textured wallpaper in a paler green, it instantly softened the room without sacrificing any of its character."

GIDEON MENDELSON

FARROW & BALL | OLIVE 13

"I gravitate toward colors that are hard to classify, like this one. It's somewhere between a Creole mustard gold and the infamous green associated with—ahem—bodily functions. Obviously a tough sell. But it's a dark-horse winner. In my family room, it picks up the botanical hues outside to create a sultry, modern take on a garden room. That chameleon quality is the secret to its success."

MELISSA RUFTY

PRATT & LAMBERT | MIDDLESTONE 12-22

"Bringing the outdoors in, like this blue that mimics the sky, is not a radical notion. What makes this shade up-to-the-minute is that it's not cozy. It captures the vastness of the sky on the cusp of autumn, as days grow chillier and colors become richer."

LILLY BUNN

BENJAMIN MOORE | FADED DENIM 795

"It seems like a noncolor, but would you believe this taupe is one of the richest, most romantic, most flattering hues around? You'll be astonished every time you see it. As the light changes throughout the day it transforms, and its mauve tones become more pronounced. For a client's apartment, it was stunning teamed with luxe leathers, shagreens, and accents of silver and bronze."

KEVIN DUMAIS

BENJAMIN MOORE | HAZELWOOD 1005

"For the closet of an über-fashionable client, I threw a curveball with this retro revival pink. It's fresh but it has a vintage quality, reminiscent of the bubble gum I loved as a kid. When I commit to vibrant I take it to the max, so I used it on everything from the trim to the shoe shelves. The best part: It's super-flattering to her complexion—and to almost anyone else's!"

ANDREW HOWARD

FARROW & BALL | NANCY'S BLUSHES 278

"Exotic, uplifting colors that inspire joy are hot right now, a reaction to all the neutrals prevalent everywhere. This is bright and vivid, like sunshine for your home. I first saw it in Jaipur, India, when I spotted a man at a festival wearing a marigold necklace. The merriment and liveliness it exuded left me almost speechless. I love it in a powder room, or in a high gloss for an entry."

FAWN GALLI

SHERWIN-WILLIAMS | GOLDFINCH SW 6905

"Growing up on a Texas ranch, I'd ride my horse into the fields, lie back in the saddle, and see this calm gray-blue above me. It works in almost any light, in almost any room, and that versatility positions it as a new neutral, alongside gray and white. With a dull lipstick red or an egg-yolk yellow, it's absolute gorgeousness."

ASHLEY DARRYL

FARROW & BALL | PARMA GRAY 27

"What this arctic-lake blue represents is so appealing right now. Calling to mind childhood days spent outside, exploring nature without parental supervision, it's about being unencumbered and free. I chose it for my daughter's bedroom to encourage her to be inquisitive, but it can also go cosmopolitan with velvet and mahogany."

MEREDITH ELLIS

C2 PAINT | ARGYLE C2-751

"I was tired of 'safe' and in search of gray's provocative alter ego for this formal living room. I wanted an evolution, with more mood and more punch, and this delivered. Containing whispers of minty greens and mercurial blues, it's like a hazy fog blurring the line between ocean and sky. A shape-shifter, it constantly astonishes and dazzles."

LAUREN NELSON

BENJAMIN MOORE | BOOTHBAY GRAY HC-165

"Years ago, John Ike—one of the partners in my firm—introduced me to James McNeill Whistler's *Peacock Room*. It was totally the opposite of what I would normally be drawn to—ostentatious, a total show-off—but it was beautiful! The color was like a deep ocean with different shades of blue and green. I want to see it used on faux-shagreen kitchen cabinets."
MIA JUNG

BENJAMIN MOORE | TEAL OCEAN 2049-30

"Mysterious and sexy, black is exciting because it's underused. Most people have never been in an all-black room—they view it as unapproachable and edgy. But the surprise is how chic and welcoming it is. As much of a blank canvas as white, it complements everything from modern Scandinavian to Italian Renaissance styles and adds intrigue to any story you're telling."

JEREMIAH BRENT

BENJAMIN MOORE | BLACK 2132-10

"This reproduction of a cobalt blue used by George Washington for Mount Vernon clearly has longevity. It's the durability—I call it history with horsepower—that makes it current. What's more modern than revisiting and sampling the past? For a young family's restored Colonial farmhouse, I paired it with 1960s lighting, klismos chairs, and suzanis. Astounding!"

JEFFREY BILHUBER

FINE PAINTS OF EUROPE | POTOMAC BLUE MV23

It's daring to use one color throughout an entire room. I've always loved Whistler's *Peacock Room*, and here peacock-blue paint covers up some dated millwork and is juxtaposed with crisp white linen fabrics and a darker blue silk rug. The intense color is sexy and dreamy. Curl up with a book and get immersed in it, and the blue."

KRISTIN HEIN

FINE PAINTS OF EUROPE | S 3040-B10G

"We're moving away from the blush hues and toward an adventurous, offbeat lilac. A mix of orchid purple and cream, it's more wacky and dangerous than where we've been, but you need fantasy in tough times. I see it in the Brooklyn loft of a secretive CIA operative. Her place is all bleached woods and matte espresso metals, with a sleek sheepskin chair from my line in this hue."

BRETT BELDOCK

BENJAMIN MOORE | ANGELINA 1376

"I have been perusing travel sites while planning a trip to celebrate my parents' birthdays, and I've been inspired by how residents of many exotic locales use fun colors on their front doors to brighten up their facades. This apple green—not quite lime or acidic—would look fantastic against a gray or white exterior."

ANNIE LOWENGART

GLIDDEN | GREEN GRAPE 88YY 66/447

"Studio Green is at the forefront of my color wheel these days. It's an incredibly deep shape-shifter of a tone. To create a moody escape in any space, I would adorn the walls with this green and couple it with light, textured fabrics on the furniture. To top it all off, I'd be sure to have some killer lighting."

MELISSA LEWIS

FARROW & BALL | STUDIO GREEN 93

"I recently fell in love with the vibrant tangerine color of a client's Hermès handbag. It's joyous, exciting, and gutsy! Orange remains one of those elusive, undiscovered countries in the world of color. Some people are ambivalent about using it because it's not safe or conservative, but it's all about how you work it in with everything else."

COREY DAMEN JENKINS

SHERWIN-WILLIAMS | OBSTINATE ORANGE SW 6884

"I'm very inspired by nature. When working out West, we are fortunate to experience the majestic Roosevelt elk in the immediate landscape of our projects. I would use the brown-gray tones of the elk's coat in a high gloss on a wall to accentuate the texture of wood and create more depth of space."

WILLIAM PEACE

FINE PAINTS OF EUROPE | E25-44

"I regret not using this dark, sexy hue—not quite gray, not quite brown— from the get-go in my Chicago apartment. I had spent years on the renovations, I was finally done, but the living room's taupe walls felt . . . off. Repainting was a revelation. The glare off Lake Michigan was tamed, the art popped, it all clicked. It was the only thing I revised in the room, but it was everything."

HOLLY HUNT

BENJAMIN MOORE | TWEED COAT CSP-85

Take a Trip Without Leaving the House

Get away every day with colors inspired by dreamy destinations and exotic locales.

"You'll see this shade of Prussian blue in butterflies, Orientalist paintings, or Turkish robes, and the way we used it in this dining room—with canary yellow and coral—feels very exotic. The lacquer finish changes the color and gives it body and depth. It glistens. The atmosphere is luxurious and rich, like a sultan's palace."
ALEX PAPACHRISTIDIS

**FINE PAINTS OF EUROPE |
DEEP SAXE BLUE BS113**

"The London restaurant Sketch Gallery made me fall in love with pink. Portola's Starman is more subtle, less public-space pow. It comes in a specialty finish called Royal Satin that has mica in it, so even though it is a blush color, it has a silvery sheen, like satin ballet slippers. I can't wait to try it in a kitchen with brass cabinet doors."

TARA SEAWRIGHT

PORTOLA PAINTS & GLAZES | STARMAN

"While visiting the Art Institute of Chicago last summer, I fell hard for this delicate violet in one of Monet's water-lily paintings. It was like a sweet melody standing out among the other colors on the canvas. It would be a perfect accent to a navy blue or charcoal gray, or as a splash of color within a neutral palette."

AMY WAX

SHERWIN-WILLIAMS | AWESOME VIOLET SW 6815

"I'm so inspired by the earth tones I see at my family's cabin on Anderson Island in Washington State. This muddy lavender is the perfect complement to the rich greens, browns, and warm grays of the Pacific Northwest. I'd use it as an adventurous neutral in a kitchen or bathroom. It would be gorgeous with walnut or smoked oak, unlacquered brass, and a beautiful marble."

HEIDI CAILLIER

FARROW & BALL | BRASSICA 271

"In California, we tend to lean toward light-colored walls, but I'm dying to use Mahogany. The color reminds me of an iconic chocolate-brown Billy Baldwin room. I think it would be a great backdrop for art and antiques—not to mention neutral upholstery. The color really pops in the evenings, especially with candles lit."
DAVID PHOENIX

FARROW & BALL | MAHOGANY 36

"I was lucky enough to have dinner once with designer Juan Pablo Molyneux and his wife in their Paris home. The cinnamon red of his library was cozy and welcoming and practically glowed in the evening light. While I may not be able to build my own secret door like the one hidden in his bookshelves, I could paint the walls in a color that transports me back to that magical night."
MELANIE CODDINGTON

C2 PAINT | TURKISH MARKET C2-571

"On my last trip to Paris, I became enamored with a door painted in this delicious, saturated magenta. It's a romantic and passionate color that brings to mind a kiss—or even gleaming, wet nail polish, freshly applied. I would love to use it in a woman's office with floor-to-ceiling built-ins. I'd give it a glossy finish and pair it with white furnishings and brass accents."
KEITH LICHTMAN

BENJAMIN MOORE | TWILIGHT MAGENTA 2074-30

"Elafonissos, a small island off the southern coast of the Peloponnese in Greece, is renowned for its pink sand beaches. It's a quiet place, almost empty, with a winsome blend of exoticism and serenity. I took the deepest shade of that pink and used it to transform the walls of a long, dark hallway, with black lacquer moldings and pale pink carpeting."

ASLER VALERO

PRATT & LAMBERT | ENCHANTRESS 3-10

"Years ago, I was very lucky to visit Marie-Hélène de Rothschild's home outside of Marrakech. It was one of the most chic interiors I've ever seen, with this fabulous yellow on the walls that was so warm and inviting. It made the eclectic mix of furniture and fabrics come out stronger. The rooms had such simplicity, in an opulent way."

MILLY DE CABROL

FARROW & BALL | CITRON 74

"Mmm. . . red! I'm glad it has moved beyond the dining room, because I adore the power and energy red brings to a space. As a child growing up in Okinawa, Japan, my favorite kimono—given to me by our Japanese gardener—was just this shade. It's oxblood, which has such depth. Paired with any blue, from cerulean to midnight, it's classic."

TRACI ZELLER

GLIDDEN | RED DELICIOUS GLR30

"This particular shade of chartreuse is a real chameleon. Alongside neutrals, it can feel soft and sensuous. But add a rich teal or a peacock blue to the mix, and you're taken to a new, exciting place. It's an unexpected color, and that makes it intriguing. You could also pop in a little charcoal to liven things up."
CAROLE WEAKS

BENJAMIN MOORE | ARTICHOKE HEARTS 382

"The touch of gray in this deep, hazy blue hints at clouds on the horizon—clouds that the captain of a tall ship would have welcomed, knowing that soon the trade winds would provide passage through the tropics. I'd use it in a small, cozy library, with lots of white trim. Or it would make a standout piece of painted furniture."
PAMELA O'BRIEN

SHERWIN-WILLIAMS | ST. BART'S SW 7614

"Elton John once handed me a flower that had a glorious pink tint and said, 'Do the room around this.' I found some lovely Colefax and Fowler chintzes, and the seating ranged from casual American wicker to sophisticated Jean-Michel Frank. And of course I carried the color onto the ceiling. Because, after all, who doesn't look good in a blush of pink?"
STAN TOPOL

BENJAMIN MOORE | QUEEN ANNE PINK HC-60

"One of my favorite things to do when I travel is to visit the local food markets, and this particular shade of red reminds me of the dried chili peppers that hang in such abundance in the outdoor stalls throughout India. Red is an energetic color that denotes power and passion. It adds a lot of impact to a room at minimal expense."

ELLIE CULLMAN

BENJAMIN MOORE | HABANERO PEPPER 1306

"This smoldering shade of pink makes me think of a Costa Rican sunset as it shimmers against the ocean. A tinge of orange keeps it from going too sweet. You could re-create that glow by using it in high gloss in a dining room. Add a Murano glass chandelier and, ta-da, you have magic!"

JOSHUA SMITH

PRATT & LAMBERT | AZALEA 5-12

"If I'm looking to get away and escape the daily chaos, I want to walk into a space that exudes tranquillity. This perfect shade of turquoise reminds me of a vacation in the Caribbean, a place where you can relax and put your feet up while all your worries are swept away. It would be very happy in a kitchen or a sunporch."

REBECCA TIER SOSKIN

BENJAMIN MOORE | UN-TEAL WE MEET AGAIN 739

"This is a romantic and charming blue with soft undertones of gray. For me, it embodies Paris in the rain—the silvery reflections on the streets, the misty sky, the coat-grabbing wind. It's a very soothing color, so I see it in either a bedroom or a breakfast room. Pair it with yellows and oranges to make the blue look even richer."

RYAN SAGHIAN

DUNN-EDWARDS PAINTS | EVEREST DRENCHED RAIN DE5883

"In Mykonos, the sea is this crystal-clear, greeny aqua that, when the sun shines on it, creates lighter and darker shades of itself. I'd apply a glaze to make it glassy and translucent. Keep the floors pale and natural, throw in some oversize furniture with white slipcovers and citrusy yellow pillows, and you'll be transported to the Aegean in no time. Ouzo helps complete the illusion."

JONATHAN ROSEN

VALSPAR | MYSTIC SEA 5007-7A

"This calm green is a mashup of my global memories. I like to stay in constant contact with nature, and it's a combination of the woods, trees, and grasses I've encountered growing up in South Africa, living in Australia, visiting Sweden, and residing in the Hamptons. No matter where I am in the world, it always creates a serene environment."

MARK ZEFF

FARROW & BALL | VERT DE TERRE 234

"The peachy orange inside a conch shell kick-started the palette of this guest bedroom in Antigua. It's an intense hue, but you can go strong in the bright sunlight of the West Indies, and it helped perk up what was once a dreary ceiling. I'm a big believer in homes relating to their surroundings, and this Caribbean color can be found just steps away on the beach."
GARY MCBOURNIE

SHERWIN-WILLIAMS | CARNIVAL SW 6892

"At an intimate dinner party in a Milanese palazzo, I fell in love with the blush hue on the walls. Ubiquitous in Tuscany, it's a wonderfully nuanced shade of peach with pink undertones—or is it pink with peach undertones? The mysteriousness makes it magical. You're drawn in and curious, and isn't that the hallmark of a fabulous interior?"

ALLISON CACCOMA

C2 PAINT | PILLOW TALK C2-514

"To me, white is the quintessential vacationy color! Think of seaside villas in Mykonos, clapboard salt-boxes in Nantucket, or a beachcomber in Maine in her white jeans and a blue-and-white top. This is the perfect pure shade of travel-inspired white. It works any- and everywhere, from the country to the city, in a rental or a grand home."

JULIE MASSUCCO KLEINER

C2 PAINT | MILK MOUSTACHE C2-692

"Imagine sailing around the Greek islands and looking into the deep teal-blue water. There's a certain sexiness you feel on your skin when you're out on a boat in the sand and the breeze, relaxed and loose. When I walk into a room painted this color, I'm completely transported. Suddenly I'm floating in the Aegean, bobbing up and down with the waves."

MARSHALL WATSON

SHERWIN WILLIAMS | GULFSTREAM SW6768

"If you've ever stood on a windsurfing board in the tropics, astounded by the vibrant color of the ocean, you know this vivid turquoise. Casual and laid-back, it brought a playfulness to this California poolhouse, sending the message to relax and hang out. I was a little nervous about such a supersaturated color at first, but I followed my gut—and it was so worth it!"
ANN LOWENGART

BENJAMIN MOORE | MEXICALI TURQUOISE 662

"As graceful as the flower for which it's named, this delicate lavender has a sweet allure. I initially saw it while traveling in London, at an exhibition of Jason Martin's abstracts. His acrylic on aluminum, *Detox*, with its shadings of blue and violet, showed me how charismatic this color could be. Surprisingly sophisticated in a room with classic pieces and sumptuous textures."

CHARLES ALLEM

BENJAMIN MOORE | FREESIA 1432

"I'm obsessed with this hypnotic, exotic cobalt. We first crossed paths in art school, when I was transfixed by Yves Klein's blues, and recently we reconnected in Marrakech. Full of life, astonishing without being aggressive, it's the most memorable color I know. A note of caution: It's all-or-nothing powerful, so use it astutely."

JEAN-LOUIS DENIOT

DUNN-EDWARDS PAINTS | DIVE IN DE5895

"As you sail the Chicago coastline, the water reflects the endless sky above. All you see is this mercurial blue with hints of smoke gray. What better color for the Windy City bedroom of a thoughtful youngster? He's an avid reader, daydreamer, and deep thinker, and his window seat looks out to Lake Michigan. Like little boys and the lake itself, it's an ever-changing hue."

ANTHONY MICHAEL

FARROW & BALL | STIFFKEY BLUE 281

"I recently stayed at a game preserve in India and slept in an open-air bed on stilts, or a machan. At night, the star-strewn sky was this exact shade of dark, soulful indigo. It can skew black in small spaces, but it's inky blue in larger rooms, especially with crisp whites. For a media room I used it in a high gloss, with gold accents and brass fixtures that evoked campfires and constellations. Amazing!"

CARMIÑA ROTH

FARROW & BALL | BLACK BLUE 95

"I'm an island boy. I was born and raised in Sumatra, and I've also spent a lot of time in Bali. This is the rich, lush green you find in the hills and forests of those places, and the boldness—and elegance— it can bring to a room is astounding. For a guesthouse in San Francisco, I partnered it with a silvery taupe chinoiserie-style wallpaper, antiques, and Asian accents."

JONATHAN RACHMAN

SHERWIN-WILLIAMS | GREENS SW 6748

"On an unforgettable trip to the boho beach town of Trancoso, Brazil, I noticed building facades painted this light green. Gorgeous against all the vegetation, it's the kind of color that would dance a samba beside lapping waves under the moonlight. I see it on the walls of an outdoor terrace with a low banquette upholstered in earthy oranges and reds and throw pillows in sea blue."

SARA BENGUR

DONALD KAUFMAN COLOR | DKC-102

"On vacation in the Caribbean islands, I was walking along a street and stopped to sit on a ledge so I could look down at the water, which was exactly this color. And suddenly, just three feet away, all these tropical fish were swimming by in the most amazing purples, yellows, and greens. We humans can make many beautiful things, but nothing is more beautiful than what's already here in nature."

ERINN VALENCICH

VALSPAR | SIGNATURE TURQUOISE TINT 5006-10B

"With this fresh green, I'm instantly whisked to my favorite Parisian park, the Jardin des Tuileries. It's as if I'm leisurely strolling along the manicured paths leading to the Louvre on a summer day. To bring out its urbane side, pair it with black lacquer and aged gold. Or try it on a ceiling— you'll feel as if you're canopied by verdant trees."

MICHAEL HEROLD

SHERWIN-WILLIAMS | LOUNGE GREEN SW 6444

"In Turkey, the sea is so clear and so bright—a true ocean blue, like this color. You see the same blue in the tiles in the Blue Mosque. It has endless depth, and that makes it very calming. I'm imagining it in a high-gloss finish in an entry or a library. After all, it's only paint. Take a risk and go for it!"

DAVID PHOENIX

GLIDDEN | PREMIUM CARIBBEAN SEA GLB02

"When you think of the color of a lake, you have to think about trees and shadows and clouds. It's muddled, like this gray-blue. It's not a clear jewel tone, like the ocean. The ocean, with its breaking waves, is all about energy. Lake water is more soothing. It laps at the shore. This gray-blue kind of washes over a room, and you don't see the clutter."

SUSAN FERRIER

FARROW & BALL | MODERN EMULSION LIGHT BLUE 22

"This has the coolness of a long, tall drink of water on a hot day. I use it frequently for ceilings because it's subtle. It catches your eye but doesn't yell. Or, if you want to dazzle, do it in high gloss on the walls, and the space will be electrified!"

JAMES HOWARD

BENJAMIN MOORE | REGAL SELECT BLUE VEIL 875

"Such a classic city color. You see it on villas throughout Rome—including mine—and everywhere in Jaipur, India. Jaipur's famous pink buildings were painted in 1876 to welcome the Prince of Wales, and the hue's longevity attests to its cosmopolitan allure. My living room has been this shade for years. Very tranquil, like a hazy sunset."

MICHELLE NUSSBAUMER

PORTOLA PAINTS & GLAZES | PARIS PINK PC 106

"There's a kind of clarity in the air after a rain, and this color has the same feeling. It suddenly makes the ceiling of a room seem taller, and the space somehow becomes larger. It totally changes the room's energy and makes you feel like you can finally take a big, deep breath!"

KATIE MAINE

FARROW & BALL | BORROWED LIGHT 235

"Some people would call this pale gray, but it actually has blue and purple in it. To me, it's the color of the fog out here in Seattle. I used it in a living room with massive windows overlooking the Pacific Ocean, and at certain times of the day, you couldn't tell the difference between the sea and the sky and the walls. They were all the same color."
BRIAN PAQUETTE

BENJAMIN MOORE | AURA EARLY FROST CSP-590

"I'm not sure if it's named for Billy Joel's bluesy ode to the Big Apple, but this dark, saturated navy is the personification of New York. Its drama can make a space feel both optimistic and brooding, which sums up Manhattan to me. I'd pair it with patinated brass and dulled silver, rich brown leathers, and mahogany antiques."
PHOEBE HOWARD

BENJAMIN MOORE | NEW YORK STATE OF MIND 805

"This icy blue has a cool crispness that's refreshing. I'd add fabrics in different tones of the same shade, like navy and slate, to create a layered, monochromatic look. Or you could bring in contrasting colors, like brown and red. The warmth and coziness of all the textures and tones make the room easy to be in."
ROBERT STILIN

PRATT & LAMBERT | ACCOLADE SMOKE RING 26-1

"This former whaler's cottage in Sag Harbor, New York, has a subtle nautical theme, and the deep, dark blue in the dining room is meant to evoke the deep, dark Atlantic, which is only a few steps from the door. The paint finish is matte to absorb as much light as possible and let the objects arranged on it shine."
TOM SCHEERER

BENJAMIN MOORE | REGAL SELECT POLO BLUE 2062-10

"Certain shades of blue immediately take me away to a tropical island, and this is one of them. Even though it's a medium-bright tone, it's still calming, yet vibrant enough to make me feel happy as soon as I enter the room. Add accents of tangerine and lime green to enhance the tropical flavor."
DEBBIE VIOLA

SHERWIN-WILLIAMS | EMERALD MAJOR BLUE 6795

"This is the deep, almost Prussian blue of the ocean in the Bahamas at low tide, and when you combine it with coral-colored fabrics, it's amazing. It vibrates in a wonderful way. I've also used it in a bedroom with blue-and-white toile. If you're doing a home anywhere near the sea or you simply want to remember the sea, this is the color to go with."
ALESSANDRA BRANCA

BENJAMIN MOORE | AURA SANTA MONICA BLUE 776

CHAPTER 3

Color Conundrums

Solutions for Tricky Spaces

Problem-Solving Colors

Boost your mood or disguise a flaw. These transformative colors are makeover magic.

"Not every room can have a dozen windows. When there's only one, like in the dining room of this Spanish-style home, you have to emphasize it! This earthy sage on the mullions and trim guides you to the view and echoes the garden outside. Repeating the color on the baseboards and bamboo chairs tied the room together."

CHRISTINE MARKATOS LOWE

FARROW & BALL | STONE WHITE 11

"One of my toughest challenges was designing a bright, happy bedroom for a young girl. The catch? The room had no windows! Zero! None! Initially, I feared a saturated color would make the space too cave-like. Then I found this pink. Yes, it's like bubble gum and Candy Land and Shirley Temple tap dancing. But it's cheerful and cozy, and it shifted the entire mood of the room."

HEATHER GARRETT

SHERWIN-WILLIAMS | PARTYTIME SW 6849

"I call this blue my miracle worker. Nothing bests it if you need fast drama and the only change you can make is the paint color. That said, it requires some confidence because it's not quiet and shy. I capitalized on its boldness for an entryway with built-in bookcases in a Manhattan apartment. Teamed with a vivid yellow on the back of the shelves, it set a tone of color fearlessness."

LAUREN MCGRATH

FARROW & BALL | OVAL ROOM BLUE 85

"An ice blue exuding tranquillity, this is my go-to for rooms lacking glamour. If it's a space with no pizzazz and no specialness, no problem—I just saturate it with this color, and it's immediately sophisticated. Because it's able to be warmed up or cooled down, it's the perfect backdrop. Pair it with silver or gold, natural woods, and almost any blues, from turquoise to gray-blue."

JONI VANDERSLICE

BENJAMIN MOORE | PALE SMOKE 1584

"You don't always have the time or the budget to refinish the floors or install the moldings you intended. My no-fail fix: Paint the ceiling this pale, subtle blue. Not only is it calming, it also diverts attention away from flaws, like a Zen master guiding you toward a different path. It's more versatile than you'd suspect. I've paired it with everything from leaf-green wallpaper to navy lacquered walls."

LESLIE BANKER

PRATT & LAMBERT | DECEMBER EVE 23-02

"Like a lot of New York City renters, I had a tiny, blah bedroom. The space cried out for energy, but it still had to be soothing. This multitasking blue—the color you see when you lie on the grass and stare at a cloudless sky—struck the perfect balance. It brought in that sense of unlimited openness and inner peace you get from gazing at and contemplating nature."

WILL TAYLOR

BEHR | TIBETAN TURQUOISE MQ4-53

"When a room doesn't get much light, people tend to reflexively reach for a super-dazzling white. But that's too flat—the absence of depth will close the room in. This grayish ivory, the misty color of morning fog, does the opposite. Layers of pigments—there are beige undertones—give a room greater complexity than a one-note hue. It took 20 attempts to find this color, but it was worth it!"

ALYSSA KAPITO

FARROW & BALL | STRONG WHITE 2001

▲

"Old-world sumptuousness was the goal for the living room of this 1920s home. Since the clients were doing a minor face-lift rather than a to-the-studs overhaul, color had to impart character. This hue, white with a soft green cast, recalls an heirloom linen you'd find in Europe, and I used it in a way that Europeans do, by painting the entire room, including the walls, ceiling, trim, and fireplace. Pure sophistication!"

MICHAEL DEL PIERO

SHERWIN-WILLIAMS | RAMIE SW 6156

"This sun-blasted yellow is F-U-N fun! In spaces that don't have much to offer, it's a mega injection of optimism and perkiness. For a quaint breakfast nook that lacked zest, I painted the walls this color and laid a lattice of white molding on top. So upbeat and fresh! But I've got to warn you: This is a nuclear yellow. Balance out its extreme energy with neutrals to tone down its pep."

BRIAN PATRICK FLYNN

SHERWIN-WILLIAMS | DAISY SW 6910

"Paint is your best friend if renovations aren't possible, but you can't be shy! Skip bland and go straight to daring, like this strong gray. I use it on the mullions of traditional colonial-style windows, and the transformation is stunning: They instantly look modern, as if they were steel casement. At night, the mullions seem to disappear into the darkness, and all you see is the view outside. Magical!"

GLENN GISSLER

FARROW & BALL | RAILINGS 31

"What to do in a study with outdated paneling that's too costly to remove? Disguise it by drenching all of the woodwork—walls, baseboards, bookshelves, crown moldings—in a glossy melted-chocolate brown. The result was luxurious and masculine, rich and lush—I'm crazy for it! It's a serious hue, but it's a counterpoint to the rest of the house, which is— surprise!—vibrant and sunny."

ADRIAN JOHNSON

SHERWIN-WILLIAMS | BLACK BEAN SW 6006

"Like the little gray dress of colors, this is understated and trend-proof—and ideal for a young brother and sister's shared bedroom, where adding a wall wasn't an option. It's neutral without being boring, and it worked with her favorite pinks and his favorite greens. It also made the space seem larger, so they could spread out, both literally and figuratively, to play, imagine, and dream."

CATE DUNNING

BENJAMIN MOORE | METROPOLITAN AF-690

"You know how good it feels to turn your face to the sun? That warm, life-giving quality is one of the things that makes yellow very healing. It's a color of hope and clear thinking. Yellow makes you feel there are possibilities. Suddenly you see things in a new light."

KATE SMITH

PRATT & LAMBERT | SHANTUNG 11-2

"Everybody is working so hard, and you want to come home to a place where you can rest. This beige may be neutral, but I swear it has medicinal, calming qualities—and it doesn't require a prescription! You'll emerge refreshed, with the energy to keep moving and creating. Bring in burnt orange, dark gray, or indigo blue."

ERIN MARTIN

FARROW & BALL | STONY GROUND 211

"There's a softness to this cream, with a touch of red, that attracts me. That bit of warmth makes it more uplifting. It's like a blossom in spring. I would do it in a bedroom with olive, navy, or eggplant. It's gentle and clean and optimistic—a fresh way of being Zen."

BRETT BELDOCK

PANTONE | DELICACY 11-2409

"This is about rebirth, growth, and nature. It's the color of new leaves. Chartreuse can be very acid, but this is more of a soft yellow-green, easy to work with. I see it in a master bedroom with creamy linens and a touch of coral. It would bring in some life."

BARRY JOHNSON

FULL SPECTRUM PAINTS | CHARTREUSE

"There's something in the color blue that triggers a relaxation response. It makes me feel as if I'm floating in a boat, looking up at the sky. Everything about it speaks of a gentle, tranquil, Zen state of mind. This is not an aloof blue. It's a blue that gathers you in."
LEATRICE EISEMAN

PANTONE | STILLWATER 16-4610

"This color envelops you, quietly penetrating like a deep massage. You can relax and regroup, physically and emotionally, until you regain your strength. It's the color of the clay pipes made by the indigenous people of our land to communicate with the creator. It doesn't feel like paint. It feels like mother earth herself."
KATHRYN SCOTT

FARROW & BALL | ETRUSCAN RED 56

"Green is in the middle of the spectrum, so in a sense it incorporates both ends and embraces all the realms of light that people need for nourishment. It evokes both warmth and coolness. Since it's ubiquitous in nature, it takes us back to nature. Try it in a guest room or a garden room, accented with white."
DONALD KAUFMAN

DONALD KAUFMAN COLOR | DKC-63

"This is on a single wall in my galley kitchen. That way you don't feel like you just fell into a berry smoothie. Violet draws out a higher consciousness, so they say, because it's nearest to black. And it's simultaneously warm and cool, vibrant and relaxed, vintage and fresh. It makes me a mellow kind of happy."
NOELLE LAKE

BENJAMIN MOORE | INSPIRED AF-595

"I've been on seven airplanes in the last eight days, and to walk into this soothing mocha would instantly make me feel grounded. Reds and browns are related to the root chakra, at the base of the spine. They're geared to stability because they're the colors of the earth. And they make you look good. They're nice next to skin."
CLODAGH

BENJAMIN MOORE | WHISPERING WOODS 1012

"Pink represents love and tenderness. It opens up the heart and increases receptivity. It attracts kindness and compassion, which is very helpful for emotional healing. It will put the sweetness back into your life."
MICHELE BERNHARDT

GLIDDEN | FRESH PINK LEMONADE GLR17

Artful Colors

Show off a time-honed collection with a deep, rich hue. It's a more effective—and alluring—backdrop than white.

"If you've ever been to one of the great old-school galleries where they show treasures against a dark red velvet wall, you know there's more to life than white. What you want when you feature paintings and drawings is not necessarily lightness but minimal distraction—and that can come from a dark, inky-brown background, which delivers a little drama as well."

DAVID NETTO

FARROW & BALL | TANNER'S BROWN 255

"In a Connecticut dining room, we painted the walls a delicate sage green to open the room to the landscape and create a calm setting for a large-scale photograph by Robert Polidori. Over the years, I've found that any color whatsoever works as a backdrop for art. White can be sterile—more gallerylike than homey—so we embrace color with a full heart!"

ELLIE CULLMAN

BENJAMIN MOORE | SPRING BUD 520

"I've done turquoise walls, orange walls, black walls, and a lot of white walls. Simplicity is in style right now, and pale gray is the new beige. It's warmer than white, so there's not so stark a contrast between the wall and a painting. And you can put anything against it, which is useful for someone who likes to change his or her art frequently."

PENNY DRUE BAIRD

BENJAMIN MOORE | METALLIC SILVER 2132-60

"After a trip to St. Barts, I painted my Dallas dining room in this perfect blend of blue and green, and I haven't changed it in 15 years. It's a great neutral, somehow both cool and warm, and every single painting I've ever put up on it looked terrific. It's an atmospheric color, very enveloping."

JAN SHOWERS

BENJAMIN MOORE | WYTHE BLUE HC-143

"Often, whites can read as too harsh. This is a softer neutral, with a hint of blue-gray that creates a soothing, calming space. It's a wonderful color to use as a backdrop and would set off any type of art beautifully."

JAMES HUNIFORD

C2 PAINT | KIND OF BLUE C2-772

"White doesn't really do anything to enhance an image, but this happy, sophisticated chartreuse acts almost like a colored matte. It frames the artwork in a way, highlighting it and pushing it out at you. Everything looks more crisp and fresh against it. Put the exact same artwork on plain white walls and it would be a little ho-hum."

TODD ALEXANDER ROMANO

BENJAMIN MOORE | ST. ELMO'S FIRE 362

"In the large foyer of a traditional Georgian house, I painted the walls an unusual color: lavender. Everything from French drawings to American oil paintings looked amazing on it, and I thought, This is the best color I've ever seen for art. It just makes everything glow. It illuminates the frames and makes the art pop."

MARY MCGEE

BENJAMIN MOORE | LAVENDER MIST 2070-60

"My approach depends on the art. If it's decorative, like these two Arts and Crafts pieces, I might pick up a color from it. This whole room is done in rich, earthy tones of rust, green, and brown. But if the art is important, then the decorating steps back, and I'd go with something neutral on the walls, so nothing competes with the art."

ALEX PAPACHRISTIDIS

FARROW & BALL | BOOK ROOM RED 50

"I just finished a house that was built specifically to showcase a major art collection, and the majority of the rooms were painted in this classic white. It worked for everything from the most sublime Picasso, a Frank Stella, and a Cy Twombly to the latest Mark Bradford."

MADELINE STUART

BENJAMIN MOORE | WHITE DOVE OC-17

"Pale pink is the perfect foil for a dark brown frame because it adds warmth and softness to a space. Plus, pink is super flattering for the visage, so your art looks good and so do you! And anything called Jazz Age is just the tops, tops, tops!"

JASON OLIVER NIXON

SHERWIN-WILLIAMS | JAZZ AGE CORAL SW 0058

"Jewelers always display their finest stones on dark velvet because the light catches the stone and not the cloth. So it is with art—light your painting and hang it on a dark, velvety aubergine wall. Then stand back and admire your gem. The view will pair well with a glass of vintage Bordeaux."

MIMI MCMAKIN

BENJAMIN MOORE | GRAPPA 1393

"This is a deep, saturated gray that gives a lot of dimension to a room, especially with white trim. I think it works particularly well with abstract art. It makes a painting feel more alive and exciting, almost as if you could step inside the canvas and immerse yourself in the colors."

HEATHER MOORE

BENJAMIN MOORE | DIOR GRAY 2133-40

"Black looks strikingly fresh to me. Once it was reserved for dungeon dwellers and the most daring *decoristas*, but now it's a glamorous neutral that just oozes chic. It glows in sunlit spaces like nobody's business and is a pristine backdrop for jewel tones, brights, and, eternally, white. Opt for an eggshell finish, which won't show every mark and fingerprint."

ELAINE GRIFFIN

VALSPAR | SIGNATURE VERY BLACK 5011-2

Wicker Furniture

Take thrifty treasures from dated to dazzling with a fresh coat of a new hue.

"My favorite wicker chair is surrounded by a jungle of greenery, so I painted it in a soft, powdery green that reminds me of the underside of a leaf. Thick, gloppy paint on this 40-year-old chair also hides some of the broken pieces. I think the reason a lot of people paint old wicker is that they can't possibly think of giving it up."

MIMI MCMAKIN

SHERWIN-WILLIAMS | GREAT GREEN SW 6430

"I have a set of wonderful old Victorian wicker, but I'm tired of white, so I'm going to paint it fuchsia. What a delicious, mouthwatering color! It makes me think of red raspberries and fresh cream."

JENNIFER GARRIGUES

**SHERWIN-WILLIAMS |
EXUBERANT PINK SW 6840**

"This green is tropical, bold, and saturated—everything I love in a color. It will revive any ailing piece of wicker, and I particularly like to use it on chairs that are under a covered veranda or loggia to add some zip to the sought-after shady spaces. Pair it with cushions and pillows in a colorful cabana stripe."

GARY MCBOURNIE

BENJAMIN MOORE | MARGARITA 2026-20

"Not remotely simple to describe, this color looks as if a pale blue sky and lichen from a tree were blended together. I just used it on a wicker table that I found for my bedroom to go against pinky-peach walls. The color brings out the table's texture and shape. And since the room opens onto a terrace, it's like bringing the outside in."

CATHERINE OLASKY

FARROW & BALL | LIGHT BLUE 22

"More of an earthy peach-shrimp-clay color than a true pink, this is a sophisticated, chameleon hue that would highlight the personality of a piece. It makes dowdy brown wicker look fresh and glowing and takes 10 years off its age. Think of it as Elizabeth Arden and Helena Rubinstein in a paint can."

JOHN LOECKE

FARROW & BALL | FOWLER PINK 39

"As a southerner, wicker is one of those things I hold sacred. Traditionally, it's painted this deep, dark green—just shy of black—that forgives dirt, showcases a great stripe, and weathers to perfection. Commonly known as French Quarter green or Charleston green, it evokes the feeling of a warm summer day on a sprawling porch with a mint julep in hand."

MELISSA RUFTY

BENJAMIN MOORE | ESSEX GREEN RME-43

"I love wicker canopy chairs, the kind that completely envelop you like a cocoon. Paint one in this vibrant blue, and it will make you feel like you're swimming in the Mediterranean. Put it in a sunroom surrounded by plants, and you'll instantly be transported to some exotic locale. Find a pair of them to double the fun."

ANGIE HRANOWSKY

PRATT & LAMBERT | NANKING BLUE 23-10

Windows and Doors

These bright and bold shades will take trims from afterthoughts to attention grabbing.

"Inspired by my travels through the Greek islands—and this fountain's tiles—I chose this romantic Aegean blue for the patio doors of a 1920s home in sun-washed Southern California. A putty-gray painted door surround and wainscoting help integrate the blue with the exterior's crisp white stucco."

THOMAS CALLAWAY

**SHERWIN-WILLIAMS |
BLUE CRUISE SW 7606**

"In a dining room with vivid blue wallpaper, I did this punchy tropical hue on the window trim and then kept going, applying it to the surrounding molding and baseboards. Very old-school glamorous and also very soothing, because it creates a monochrome effect. It's my go-to trick for lowering the visual noise in a space with strong colors."

TY LARKINS

BENJAMIN MOORE | AZURE WATER 677

"You never know where a closed door might lead. Painted this rich military-uniform blue, it's like a promise that something unique is waiting behind it. It's aristocratic and proper, so maybe Mr. Darcy? Or an elegant traveler, just returned from crisscrossing the Mediterranean in his sleek sailboat? Who wouldn't open that door?"

TODD BLACK

FINE PAINTS OF EUROPE | E25-63

"After a recent trip to Mexico City, I'm obsessed with Mexican architect Luis Barragán and his favorite shade of bright pink. A hot magenta grounded by ashy undertones, it's not a color found in nature but rather in our memory of nature. On the front door of a minimal, modern building, it would be a confident punctuation mark, softening the harsh shapes and angles."

OLIVER M. FURTH

KT.COLOR | HOT MAGENTA 06.001

"Playful without being childish, this vibrant wildflower yellow on the entry door of a San Francisco Victorian instantly boosted the curb appeal. Not only did it pop against the navy-blue exterior, but it also reflected the homeowner's sophisticated contemporary style. It's a fun and friendly daily reminder not to sweat the small stuff."

REGAN BAKER

FINE PAINTS OF EUROPE | H01610

"A distinctive entrance can have a huge impact, and that was especially true for a harbor home I designed near Cape Cod. Because nearly all the front doors in the areas are white, I went with this dark slate. The blue of the deepest, clearest sea, it nods to the ocean and gives a warm welcome to visitors, who can easily spot it from the street."

DOUGLAS WRIGHT

BENJAMIN MOORE | NORTH SEA CC-932

"The delicate, whispery blue of a seeded eucalyptus or a succulent leaf, this is fresh and alive, and it alludes to new beginnings. What could be better for a front door, which is, after all, a prelude? It's gorgeous on my clients' 1920s brick Colonial with a slate roof and leaded-glass windows. They worried that judgy neighbors would express opinions about it, and they did—but it was all positive."

GEORGIA ZIKAS

BENJAMIN MOORE | GOSSAMER BLUE 2123-40

"This dining room beguiles you, like a hypnotic garden. Sinuous quince branches on the wallpaper set the scene, but it's the vivid enameled green doors that inject the danger. Glistening like the scales of a viper, they introduce a sense of secretive, forbidden passion. I could imagine a seductress entertaining paramours here."

CATHERINE BROWN PATERSON

FINE PAINTS OF EUROPE | LINDEN BS12E53

"As a first impression, a front door telegraphs your personality to the world, and this spoke volumes about my client, a best-selling author. Somewhere between a robin's-egg and a duck's-egg blue—although it's probably closest to an Ameraucana-chicken egg—its coziness and tranquillity capture her spirit. It says she's quietly confident and gracious, and happy to invite you into her home."

BETH WEBB

FARROW & BALL | LIGHT BLUE 22

"For facades, I believe the front door should wear the color, rather than the other way around. This strong and subtle red, which I used for a home in Atlanta, is the perfect example. Echoing the hues of the antique brick exterior, it is self-assured and humble, and sings rather than shouts."

PETER BLOCK

FARROW & BALL | INCARNADINE 248

Living Large

Tackle jumbo-size spaces with shades that hold their own even on the biggest scale.

"The billiard room of this 1920s Spanish Colonial Revival home was vast and plain with 14-foot ceilings. It called out for a hue rich in character to counter the size, but not so moody it would read as foreboding. This sensual blue delivered: comforting yet mysterious, with a depth to match the bold cement tiles and Moroccan light fixture."
THOMAS CALLAWAY

FINE PAINTS OF EUROPE | NCS S 2020-R90B

"This gray is shadowy, with cool violet undertones and a touch of luminosity—the color of a bespoke wool satin suit. I used it for a dramatic formal entry with a black-and-white marble floor and twin half-circle staircases. It accentuates the architecture without stealing the show. A common-area color that's anything but common!"

JEFF ANDREWS

DONALD KAUFMAN COLOR | BEACH GRASS GRAY

"How do you make a colossal space seem airy by day and cozy at night? For a client's newly built home, where all of the first-floor rooms flowed together, the answer was this elusive hue. When the sun pours in, it's a subtle blue. By evening, it transforms into a gentle gray, very family-friendly and homey without being dark—and perfect for the living and dining rooms."

KEN KEHOE

RESTORATION HARDWARE | LIGHT SILVER SAGE

"This classic yellow would make any room cheerful. It absorbs the light and bounces it right back, so when the sun shines, it absolutely glows. Yellow is a tricky color, and this is one of a handful that I use. It works because it looks beautiful—and it makes people look beautiful, too."

MICHAEL WHALEY

FINE PAINTS OF EUROPE | IVORY PALM 6012P

"Sometimes a space can appear gigantic, even if the actual square footage is not. A client's home office had a sweeping view of the garden: The sight lines kept going, and the room seemed boundless. My solution was this sexy and smoldering cinnabar red. Applied in a high gloss to the built-in bookcase behind her desk, it pulled her back into the world of work."

WILLIAM W. STUBBS

SHERWIN-WILLIAMS | BOLERO SW 7600

"Not a true white or a true cream, this is like the slightly tea-tinged interior of your grandmum's favorite china cup. It's stellar at reflecting and diffusing light, especially in a two-story great room with huge windows. The neutral hue also draws attention away from super-tall ceilings— you just see the room as a harmonious, unified space."

SHAZALYNN CAVIN-WINFREY

MYLANDS | HOLLAND PARK NO. 5

"Wide-open spaces need dimension and definition. My trick for creating those: variations on the same hue. I started with this fresh celadon in the main living area, then I added two shades of green in the adjoining rooms—one darker, one lighter, all from the same paint strip. The effect is a glamorous layering of progressive greens."

BARCLAY BUTERA

BENJAMIN MOORE | ITALIAN ICE GREEN 2035-70

▲

"An unadulterated white with no undertones—like freshly fallen snow—was my choice for the great room of this Tudor. The architecture is traditional, but with the pure white, it appears more contemporary. All that white makes the walls and ceilings recede and vanish, leaving you with a wonderful sense of intimacy in front of the fireplace."

LINDSAY CHAMBERS

FARROW & BALL | ALL WHITE 2005

"This adaptable blue-gray is the Meryl Streep of color. Multilayered and complex, it achieves the almost impossible: It makes a mammoth room feel both endless and enveloping. By bringing the walls in a bit, it gave a bedroom with tons of volume a soothing feeling without losing any sense of spaciousness. I've even painted it on kitchen cabinets, and it works its magic there, too."

CHRIS BARRETT

C2 PAINT | OVERCAST C2-738

"To me, there's nothing worse than a room with a stratospheric ceiling that isn't scaled for humans. When I want an overwhelming space to feel snug, I reach for this deep green. It's the chromatic equivalent of being wrapped in a fuzzy and sumptuous alpaca blanket."

JAN SHOWERS

PORTOLA PAINTS & GLAZES | FOUNTAIN STONE PC306

"Normally I'm the queen of explosive color. But sometimes a room needs me to dial it back. Not wanting a loud hue to fight the majesty of an entry with a floating curved staircase, I opted for this muted silver gray. The trim is a crisp, contrasting white. You walk in, and the elegance is jaw-dropping. Sometimes quiet can be as spectacular as high-wattage."

JULIA BUCKINGHAM

SHERWIN-WILLIAMS | REQUISITE GRAY SW 7023

Shine Bright

In sunny rooms, go with the warmth or temper it with colors that range from bright to soothing.

"This beautiful blue-green is one of the most multidimensional colors I have ever seen. In a space with lots of natural light, it registers as more green. Then, as the sun goes down, it appears bluer. I love that metamorphosis. It makes a room so intriguing."

TY LARKINS

FARROW & BALL | CHAPPELL GREEN 83

"This is magic-hour blue, that moment in between daylight and twilight before the color gradually fades out of the sky. It's a layered shade that captures the violet spectrum of blue yet never turns frigid. Silver sparkles against it, gold gleams, and mahogany takes on a glow. It's a saturated yet tranquil blue that may be the precise shade of heaven."

MARSHALL WATSON

FARROW & BALL | LULWORTH BLUE 89

"I've always loved deep blues, the darker the better—rich, saturated blues that complement everything around them. Last year, I used this in a showhouse and became obsessed with it. In every light, it looks different. To me, elegance means luxurious, stylish, sophisticated, and understated. You know it when you see it. No bling, just beautiful!"

KERRY DELROSE

FARROW & BALL | BLACK BLUE 95

"When the sun hits a wall, it takes the color down a notch or two. But this dark teal blue, with undertones of gray and green, is dark enough that it still looks rich and interesting. I used it on the sunporch of a 1920s Dutch Colonial, where it was a nice complement to terra-cotta floors. The unexpected color draws you into the room."

JOAN ENGER

SHERWIN-WILLIAMS | STILL WATER SW 6223

"Here in the South, a sunny room can quickly get blazing hot. Texans will do anything to escape the heat, including enveloping a room in a dark color to drop its visual temperature. This navy blue evokes a cool and peaceful starry night sky. It's deep enough not to get washed out by the sun and matte enough to absorb the light."

EMILY LARKIN

BENJAMIN MOORE | HALE NAVY HC-154

"This rich and versatile cream is my go-to hue, especially when it comes to decorating sun-drenched spaces. A pure white would be too sharp, but this picks up on the softer qualities of daylight. It subtly changes throughout the day and envelops a room in warmth at night."

SUZANNE TUCKER

BENJAMIN MOORE | SAN DIEGO CREAM 921

"In the Mississippi Delta, the sun can be overpowering at midday, when my client is in her study. So I painted the walls, moldings, and bookcases in this flint gray, a true gray that doesn't go purple or blue. With bleached floors, a white ceiling, and Belgian linen on the furniture, the room feels cool and calm."

NANCY PRICE

BENJAMIN MOORE | TEMPTATION 1609

"I'll often use this Yves Klein blue to dramatize a room. Paint it on one wall and you are instantly transported to an island in Greece, where you'll see this hue in the water and on window frames against whitewashed walls. It makes me feel as if I'm basking in the sun."

ROGER DE CABROL

BENJAMIN MOORE | EVENING BLUE 2066-20

"This is a brilliant green, deeper than chartreuse. It's kind of like sunlight through a leaf. And it comes as a surprise in the library of an apartment in an all-glass skyscraper, where the rest of the rooms are fairly beige. It reminds you of the grass and the greenery outside."

DAVID MANN

SHERWIN-WILLIAMS | HIGH STRUNG SW 6705

"I like a light but bright color in a sunny room. This yellow-green is so refreshing and crisp, you almost feel as if you're sipping a lime daiquiri by the pool! And like rum, it mixes well with anything. Pair it with navy blue to go preppy, pink to go bold, or chocolate brown to tone it down."

PHOEBE HOWARD

BENJAMIN MOORE | LIME RICKY 393

"Yellow can be tricky. It's incredibly easy to choose the wrong hue—before you know it, the walls are pale and washed out or high-wattage. This buttery shade is just right and makes a perfectly soft backdrop, day or night. In sunlight, it maintains its subtleness without looking tart, and in the evening, its richness is enveloping. For a yellow, that's the sought-after holy grail."

TODD KLEIN

BENJAMIN MOORE | AURA 169

Small Spaces

Light and bright can help—but so can rich, saturated color. Because who doesn't want a little jewel box of their own?

"I choose this pale aqua for a tiny studio—less than 300 square feet—in downtown Brooklyn. Painting it white or beige would have just screamed 'rental.' This is a happy, clear color that looks pretty on both bright summer days and throughout the dreary New York winter. And the client and I are both water signs, so the color felt apropos!"

NICK OLSEN

BENJAMIN MOORE | OCEAN SPRAY 2047-60

"I think powder rooms should be like jewelry boxes—a tiny space that gives you a precious experience. This purple with an undertone of red would make it feel as if you'd lined the room in velvet. Add a Chinese red-lacquer vanity with a polished marble top, a gilt mirror, and two gilt-and-crystal sconces for a regal look."
JOSÉ SOLÍS BETANCOURT

FARROW & BALL | FULL GLOSS BRINJAL 222

"I love bold color and, in my opinion, room size should not limit your palette. In a studio apartment, we chose this deep cerulean blue because it was vibrant, but at the same time peaceful and relaxing. Moroccan tile in blue, red, green, and yellow bordered the wood floor, and we used the yellow tones as inspiration for the fabrics."
CARL D'AQUINO

BENJAMIN MOORE | AURA SAILOR'S SEA BLUE 2063-40

"I used this on the wood-paneled walls in a small book-lined study. Crazy how this odd pea-soupy hue bathed the room in sunlight, even on the grayest day. I added an upholstered chair in a clashing shade of dark-green-on-oyster toile, an Oushak rug in burnt oranges and browns, and a sofa in a nubby pumpkin-color weave."
ROBIN BELL

FARROW & BALL |
ESTATE EGGSHELL CHURLISH GREEN 251

"Some grays are battleship cold, but this is not. It's warm and intimate. It reminds me of a very good men's suit. I'd do the trim in white, and the upholstery in shades of gray silk and linen velvet. Bring in a polished-nickel mirror, an ebony side table. All the color in the room would come from the art."

HEATHER MOORE

BENJAMIN MOORE | AURA CHELSEA GRAY HC-168

"In my country house, I turned a stair landing into a special place where I could sit and watch the sun set. The paint color—a light mossy green with a bit of gray in it—comes from the trees outside. I thought it would blend in with the foliage in summer. And in winter, when it's icy and dreary, it reminds me that spring is on the way."

MATTHEW PATRICK SMYTH

VALSPAR | SIGNATURE SPARKLING SAGE 5005-3B

"Not too yellow and not too red, this orange feels good, just like my favorite cashmere sweater. I used it as an accent wall in a guest room for a bold statement, yet it was also warm and flattering to every skin type. People felt pampered and chic, inspiring dreams of shopping at Hermès in Paris and taking home goodies in those iconic orange boxes!"

KELLEY PROXMIRE

**BENJAMIN MOORE |
REGAL SELECT ORANGE PARROT 2169-20**

"I'm obsessed with this deep purple with chocolate undertones. It's the kind of color that reveals itself in different ways, depending on the light. People think using a dark color in a small room makes it seem smaller, but that's a myth. If you do everything in it—walls and trim—the boundaries get blurred and you can't see where the room ends."

JEFF ANDREWS

SHERWIN-WILLIAMS | EMERALD RAISIN SW 7630

"My philosophy is, the smaller the space, the darker the shade. I recently used this charcoal in a powder room from floor to ceiling. It's modern and sophisticated, yet still cozy and chic. And don't be afraid of using oversize artwork in tight quarters, either. It makes the space seem bigger than it really is!"

HILLARY THOMAS

FARROW & BALL | ESTATE EGGSHELL DOWN PIPE 26

"Imagine opening the front door and seeing this bright kelly green in a high-lacquer finish. It's fun and unexpected. Or it would be amazing in a bedroom, with white bedding and white furniture. It would make a small room feel special. Be fearless and add hot fuchsia, orange, or teal."

GREGORY MCGUIRE

BENJAMIN MOORE | ADVANCE KELLY GREEN 2037-30

"In a small room, my instinct is always to go jewellike. This dark peacock blue is one of my favorites, especially when it's on all of the millwork as well as the walls. A gloss finish makes it feel instantly grand. Add a drippy chandelier and a pair of chairs covered in platinum leather for martini sipping."

HEATHER GARRETT

BENJAMIN MOORE | ULTRA SPEC 500 OASIS BLUE 2049-40

"This is a small space off the family room that we set up for the kids to do their homework. Yellow is not a color I use much, but this is a gentle yellow, more like straw. It's fun for the kids but it doesn't look juvenile. Shelves show off their artwork, and we covered a bulletin board in bright fabric. When the mirrored doors are open, it's chic and surprising."

SUZANNE KASLER

**GLIDDEN |
PREMIUM COLLECTION CRISP GINGER ALE GLY24**

"A small room is the perfect opportunity to embrace a color you're scared of—you don't have to make a huge commitment. I'd use this dark, moody blue on both the walls and woodwork. Then, on the ceiling, mix it with white in a one-to-three ratio so that the color continues across every surface."

CARI GIANNOULIAS

FINE PAINTS OF EUROPE | WC-90

Vamp It Up

Fall in love with a color that gets your heart racing. A flirty hue awaits.

"This warm, calming pink, the shade of faded peony petals or the edges of a fiery sunset, had me at hello. Not too juvenile or too twee or too sweet, it acts like a neutral. In this library, its sophisticated undertones balance all the millwork and the hand-blocked linens. It makes you want to curl up, relax, and luxuriate on the window seat."

LISA THARP

FINE PAINTS OF EUROPE | WINDSOR PINK

"I've adored this putty-blush color for as long as I can remember. It's a very emotion-steeped hue evocative of my childhood: It reminds me of quiet moments helping my mother put together her evening outfits, the ritual of choosing clothes and jewelry. Now I appreciate how it softens a room, giving it a hushed intimacy and a chic essence, and I return to its specialness constantly."

RICHARD OUELLETTE

BENJAMIN MOORE | FOGGY MORNING 2106-70

"When I was a design student, I came across a photo of a Billy Baldwin room lacquered in this masculine brown, and I was a goner. So different from the 'pretty' colors I had been working with, it pulled me in and has never let me go. I've paired it with Hermès orange, pale blue, and pink, introduced clients to it, and even used it myself. I just repainted my home office in it—again."

SHELLEY JOHNSTONE

BENJAMIN MOORE | CHOCOLATE CANDY BROWN 2107-10

"A few years ago, I spied this color on the library walls at an English country house and—boom!—immediate attraction. Confident and poised, it's a complex green that envelops you like a luxe cashmere blanket. In my new-build condo, it gave the dining and living rooms a richness and a history. Whenever anyone saw the rooms, the reaction was always the same: a dropped jaw, silence, then 'Wow!'"

WARE PORTER

FINE PAINTS OF EUROPE | E7-53

"This is an almost black, charcoal gray that has enough brown in it to keep it warm. It looks like all of those colors, depending on how the light strikes it. I like it with the drama of a white glass chandelir and silver or gold metallic accents to give it that black-tie dressiness. It's a sexy color. Try it in a semigloss, which adds depth and reflectivity."

PATRICK SUTTON

BENJAMIN MOORE | IRON MOUNTAIN 2134-30

"My relationship with this acidic green started a quarter century ago. I recognized how independent and gutsy it was in the 1990s, and I never wavered. For my dining room I went all in, but it's also fantastic in modest doses and surprisingly approachable. With indigo blue or a cantaloupe color, it feels totally current."

AMELIA HANDEGAN

BENJAMIN MOORE | SAVANNAH MOSS 385

"It's hard to pinpoint exactly what shade of blue this is, which is why it has always mesmerized me. I prefer hazy in-between colors that are hard to define. A description that comes close is of an antique French chest that was once bright blue but has gradually faded and aged—beautifully—over decades. Bring in grays, plums, and tangerines, and it's beyond gorgeous."

BRITTANY STILES

FARROW & BALL | LIGHT BLUE 22

"I go way back with this intriguing blue-green: I wore it for my senior portrait in high school! It's one of the few colors I'm drawn to that isn't inspired by nature, unapologetically clean and modern. In the kitchen of my apartment, I combined it with geometric wallpaper and pure whites. If I were actually inclined to cook, I'd be thrilled doing it around this unusual hue."

MELANIE CODDINGTON

C2 PAINT | POND SHIMMER BD-24

"The intensity and ambiguity of this unique color has enthralled me forever. Marrying my two favorite hues, blue and green, its depth makes it almost impossible to nail down—and is the reason it can be teamed with almost any textile. It recalls the soulful greens and blues Van Gogh painted again and again, which are still relevant today. Timelessness is a hallmark of nuanced colors like this."

BRYNN OLSON

FARROW & BALL | HAGUE BLUE 30

"There's a dreamy and wispy quality to this Cape Cod blue, the misty color along the New England shoreline on overcast days. I'm infatuated with it because even though it's subtle, it still packs a wallop—like a wave with an undertow. The way it instantly brings a room to life is uncanny, especially if it's a small space in need of oomph. It's unbeatable with emerald green."
EMILY CASTLE

SHERWIN-WILLIAMS | NORTH STAR SW 6246

"Surprisingly complex, this strikes a balance between delicate and strong. For a recent beach house project, we combined it with John Robshaw textiles, mirrored bedside tables, and apple-green gourd lamps. This was a small bedroom with just one window, but when sunlight hits the space, it absolutely glows."
BETHANY CASSELL VANN

BENJAMIN MOORE | SPRING LILAC 1388

"I love that this ashy lilac seems washed-out, as if it slowly faded over time to a pale whisper of what it once was. Serene and tranquil, it works well with creams, charcoals, and taupes and is ideal for a master bedroom. The gray tint lulls you to sleep in the evening and provides warmth in dawn's morning light."
DANE AUSTIN

SHERWIN-WILLIAMS | QUEEN ANNE LILAC SW 0021

"This is about glamour, glamour, glamour. And fashion—it's a mauve you usually only see in satin, as if a mercury silver was overlaid with the palest blush pink and a hint of blue and brown. So wonderful in a Paris apartment with modern pieces from Hervé Van der Straeten, vintage Maison Jansen furniture, and acres of smoky mink-colored silk velvets."

VEERE GRENNEY

FARROW & BALL | PEIGNOIR 286

"Pink undertones make this soothing, but my client was worried it could be too feminine for her den. Doing it in a high gloss on the walls, woodwork, and ceiling, and introducing masculine elements like an aged iron sconce with fractured glass, changed her mind— and mine. The end result was so dramatic and bold, I'm now more inclined to use purple in my designs."

NATALIE KRAIEM

FARROW & BALL | BRASSICA 271

"I fell for this elegant, subtle hue years ago on a buying trip to Paris. Shopping on Avenue Montaigne, I came upon the Dior boutique and was immediately smitten by the soft lavender-gray of the storefront. Seductive and timeless, with a touch of French blue, it's been in my inspiration file—and my heart—ever since."

OHARA DAVIES-GAETANO

SHERWIN-WILLIAMS | DAYDREAM SW 6541

"To me, this says luxury and ambition. It's perfect for a home office or study, because it creates a comfortable environment that encourages you to work hard and succeed. There's some black and deep indigo mixed in, which gives it seriousness, but it's also a little bit sassy."

REBECCA TIER SOSKIN

BENJAMIN MOORE | DARK LILAC 2070-30

"Inspired by imperial robes worn by the ancient Phoenicians, this deep, rich shade turned a Manhattan dining room into a multipurpose salon. Lined with books, the space is a jewel box where the envelope-pushing, well-traveled clients can spend the day reading, then entertain guests with lavish meals and fascinating conversation at night."

PHILLIP THOMAS

FINE PAINTS OF EUROPE | H04320

▼

"Like a resolute woman who gets what she wants without anyone noticing that she's getting her own way, this is understated and dignified. It's sensational paired with bright citrus greens, saturated pinks, and aquas, but it can skew blue in certain light. True story: A client's husband saw it for the first time on the living room walls and exclaimed, 'I love this blue!'"

ELIZABETH PYNE SINGER

SHERWIN-WILLIAMS | ELATION SW 6827

"Almost black in low light, this is a cross between a dark-roasted coffee bean and a ripe acai berry. It's regal but also . . . slightly insane. That edginess was what a client's stodgy, dad-style office needed. Painting the mahogany paneling and adding a Brutalist brass chandelier transformed it into a much more exciting space."

TRIP HAENISCH

FARROW & BALL | PELT 254

"Cue the James Bond music! This adrenalized purple has all the sophistication and daring of a luxury-obsessed international jewel thief in pursuit of the world's rarest gems. It's a risk-taker, a statement maker, and a b-o-s-s. In a living room where I was channeling a contemporary version of *Downton Abbey*, it delivered the goods, instantly creating an aristocratic vibe. Breathtaking!"

MICHEL SMITH BOYD

SHERWIN-WILLIAMS | DEWBERRY SW 6552

"For a time I lived in Provence, France, where lavender grows in abundance. This recalls the lighter-hued blossoms I saw there, although it's creamier—the color is closer to lavender-flavored ice cream. Approachable and contemplative, it's a gateway shade for clients hesitant about purple."

KENDALL WILKINSON

BENJAMIN MOORE | ICED LAVENDER 1410

"Mysterious, velvety, and potent, this isn't for sissies. Best suited to the powerful, the adventurous, and the seekers of spiritual wisdom and earthly luxury, it brings out my inner empress and wanderlusting mystic. It's the color of the precious amethyst held sacred by the Buddha and the sails on Cleopatra's legendary sloop—I'd do it in a high gloss in the dining room of a fiercely driven fashion type."

KATIE LEEDE

BENJAMIN MOORE | CENTURY® ACAÍ R8

Feel Cozy

With a room this restful, you won't even miss the fireplace.

"For the library of a 1906 Victorian-style home, I wanted a sense of intimacy and gravitas. Once I saw this deep aubergine, with its refinement and mystery, I knew it would ground the space. With the vintage leather chair, woolly pillow, and bespoke mirror, it's soothing and snug, as if you're having a light-night Cognac at a favorite watering hole."

RENA CHERNY

FINE PAINTS OF EUROPE | G17140

"At first glance, this creamy butter yellow—the exact shade of a Studebaker my family had when I was growing up—appears quite bright. But there's a depth beyond that initial impression. It has a hushed, meditative side to it, like an extroverted introvert. A rare combo of relaxing and cheerful, it's more likable to me than other yellows."

CARL D'AQUINO

DONALD KAUFMAN COLOR | DKC-42

"Raw umber in this Parisian pink counters its sweetness. It's balance, making it very centering. I'd compare it to a lazy afternoon in the City of Light, as you sip rosé and Edith Piaf wafts through the window. Team it with animal prints, vermilion, and chartreuse—both the color and the libation. The best part: It makes any complexion look *magnifique!*"

RAUN THORP

FARROW & BALL | PINK GROUND 202

"You get an instant drop in blood pressure with this sand-pebble hue. Tinged with gray, it's timeless and organic—it would blend right into the colors on the ocean floor. Bring in a large-scale sofa, in navy-blue mohair, some pops of orange, and touchable oversize weaves, and it would be extraordinary."

JILL GOLDBERG

PORTOLA PAINTS & GLAZES | STONE 1

"I wrapped a bedroom's walls in this restful combination of sea green and silver gray, then introduced creams, ivories, and whites. The result was like drifting off to sleep under the canopied branches of a perfect shade tree. Romantic and expressive, it's a hue you'd spot from a hillside in Provence, France."

JENN FELDMAN

PORTOLA PAINTS & GLAZES | FALLING TIDE 087

"Walk into a room painted in this barely there hydrangea blue and a sense of tranquillity washes over you. You'll immediately want to slip on flip-flops—or kick them off entirely! While it's a classic choice for a shore house, the gray undertones make it sophisticated enough to venture inland, too."

AUSTIN HANDLER

SHERWIN-WILLIAMS | MISTY SW 6232

"When I see this pale putty gray, I'm transported to the beach on a misty morning. The sand is damp, fog shrouds the weathered cedar shingles of the cottages, and everything is muted. In a room, it's complete coziness. I love the way it responds to blacks and super-saturated charcoals, and to a sexy metallic wallpaper in a city entry hall I designed."

DAN SCOTTI

BENJAMIN MOORE | STONINGTON GRAY HC-170

"Even if you're nowhere near a beach or a blue sky, this color would remind you of something out of nature. It's like sea foam—a blue-green with a powdery gray undertone. It makes me feel happy and calm at the same time. Layer it with bold navy and bright white. I might add a touch of fuchsia or lemon."

ERICA DOMESEK

GLIDDEN | ICY TEAL 50GG 55/049

"To counteract the stress of urban life, you want to be soothed. This has a peacefulness, like pulling the sunlit sky into a room. It's mercurial—I'd describe it as the quiet blue behind wispy streaks of clouds you spy from your airplane window—and it works equally well with midcentury and Swedish styles."

VICENTE WOLF

PPG PITTSBURGH PAINTS | BLUE DOLPHIN 1041-4

"The darkness and richness of this smoky gray reminds me of a luxuriant cashmere sweater. You just want to snuggle into it with a good book—and what's more serene than that? Set it in a room with plaid fabrics and saddle leathers, and you can almost smell the fire crackling in the hearth."

DAN MAZZARINI

BENJAMIN MOORE | KENDALL CHARCOAL HC-166

"This pensive, elusive blue shifts down the whole of my being into first gear, slowing the tempo of my heart. It's the layers that draw me in and send me into a reverie. Slightly green, barely gray, it causes me to ponder and wonder until I've tapped into something larger. By connecting with the impossible-to-comprehend, I forget life's mundanity and remember how lovely and miraculous it can all be."

MONA ROSS BERMAN

FARROW & BALL | OVAL ROOM BLUE 85

"To me, being Zen is about clearing your mind, and nothing does that like white—the purity, the clean-slate newness. While some shades skew chilly, the subtle lilac undertones here give warmth. It's like the buildings in Santorini: By day, they're white, but at dusk, they reflect the lavenders and pinks of the fading rays. Who wouldn't want a room like a Greek sunset?"

OLIVIA ERWIN ROSENTHAL

FARROW & BALL | GREAT WHITE 2006

"If you need a color you can trust, one that's modern without being gold, turn to this calm greige. A great unifier, it's a placid backdrop for blending both neutrals and brights. Pair it with blues, reds, and oranges, as well as contemporary art—which is exactly what I did in the living room of my home in the Hamptons. The mix feels cohesive, not jarring."

DAVID SCOTT

SHERWIN-WILLIAMS | NATURAL TAN SW 7567

"There's something comforting about this tawny brown, as if my grandfather had been in the room before I entered, puffing on his cigar. Maybe that's why it also evokes the tobacco-stained walls of a 19th-century men's club. For a Connecticut home worlds away from the city, it pulls together the laid-back mix of contemporary photos and antiques and invites you to relax."

PHILIP GORRIVAN

C2 PAINT | BUCKAROO C2-615

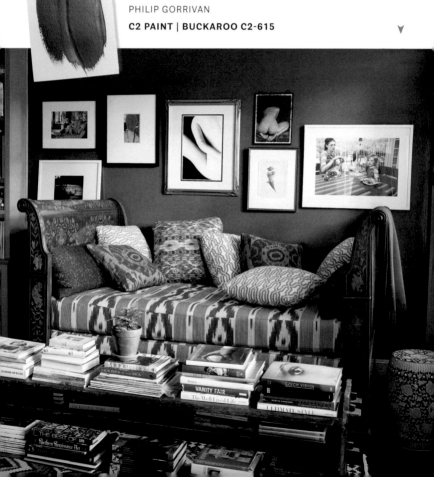

"Imagine fields of billowing wheat on the Great Plains, or the honest simplicity of a burlap sack. That's this understated heritage tan. It has a presence, but it's a gentle one, so it won't overwhelm a room. Nothing bests it for showcasing rough-hewn, hand-planed wood and earth tones."

GARROW KEDIGIAN

DONALD KAUFMAN COLOR | DKC-09

"This is a barely there Miss Havisham pink. I wasn't sure it even existed. I just knew that, for the double parlor of my Victorian cottage, I wanted a color to mimic the way early evening light softly glazes the wall. This was a revelation: The paleness pulls together the vintage leather club chairs, the scroll-arm plaid sofa, and the antique Khotan rug. I've dubbed it the grande dame of pink."

KEN FULK

FARROW & BALL | SETTING PLASTER 231

"I began associating red with rural settings during the summers I spent on my grandparents' Alabama farm. It was the color of ripe tomatoes, checked café curtains, geraniums, and my grandfather's pickup truck. This happy red captures the essence of those childhood memories. Great for a welcoming front door or a patriotic Fourth of July picnic table."

PHOEBE HOWARD

FINE PAINTS OF EUROPE | POST OFFICE RED BS 0006

"In homes far from honking taxis and busy sidewalks, I gravitate toward organic hues that echo the outdoors. This forest-inspired gray, the color of craggy stones, reminds me of trail hiking on autumn afternoons. Pair it with crisp whites, and layer in lush fabrics like suede and mohair to create coziness."

VICENTE WOLF

PPG PITTSBURGH PAINTS | DOVER GRAY 1001-5

"I'm drawn to this pine green because it whisks me away to the rolling hills of the Swiss countryside. There's an appealing tinge of blue in it that turns it into a neutral. I've relied on it again and again, for lacquered libraries, kitchen cabinets, and the front door of a manor house. Use it and you instantly connect with Mother Nature."

MICHELLE NUSSBAUMER

FINE PAINTS OF EUROPE | E13-15

"Blue is one of those colors that just happens to flatter every skin tone, from ivory to dark as pumpernickel. I don't know why—is it because it's so prevalent in nature? Studies have shown that blue also helps your ability to focus. It's a calming color, which is why I used it in my living room. This particular shade has a little gray in it, which makes it even more soothing."

SHEILA BRIDGES

FARROW & BALL | OVAL ROOM BLUE 85

"Most people think of peach as the most flattering color, but I like something with more guts. This bright burnt orange would make anyone look radiant. It would be gorgeous in a powder room or a dining room with gold, gray, or even navy. But here's the real secret—there are no rules. Just pick whatever color you like, and that will make you feel good and look wonderful."

GEOFFREY DE SOUSA

SHERWIN-WILLIAMS | YAM SW 6643

"Like a true blonde—and those who want to be one—this pale blue-green is complex and enchanting. Throughout the day, it changes from robin's-egg blue to gray-green, radiating a subtle glow that makes both people and furnishings look like the best versions of themselves. Pair it with moss-green velvet upholstery, modern art, and black-lacquer chinoiserie."

SARAH BARTHOLOMEW

FARROW & BALL | PALE POWDER 204

"Somber yet striking, dusty teals are in vogue right now, both in fashion and home. In an eggshell finish, they look calm and serene but can turn dramatic in high gloss. Add warm woods and rich caramel velvet. A touch of white helps keep the look crisp and smart."

STACEY TESTA

SHERWIN-WILLIAMS | TEMPE STAR SW 6229

"You know how great everyone looks in the Caribbean? Just bring that sunlit water into a room with this luscious aqua. It's one of those colors that can swing so many ways. Make it classic with white trim and mahogany furniture, or pop some yellow or purple against it and go modern and sassy. It makes me feel so good that I don't even bother with makeup."

ALEXA STEVENSON

BENJAMIN MOORE | GULF STREAM 670

"I'm just back from Paris, and this green was everywhere—on people in the street, on the accessories and furniture in the antiques shops on the Rue Jacob, and even at the flea market. Imagine how great it would look in a dining room. It would really set off a face, as well as a painting. Do it in lacquer for a beautiful sheen."

SUZANNE KASLER

GLIDDEN | DEEP FOREST PINE 30GG 09/106

"Aqua is a calming color, which balances a fiery redhead like myself and makes for a pretty room. Actually, most people look good in aqua, and when you look good, you feel more confident. I often like to use a range of one color, so I might add a darker teal or Prussian blue. Red or pink would punch it up and give it more pizzazz."

LINDSEY CORAL HARPER

BENJAMIN MOORE | ANTIGUAN SKY 2040-60

"I find it relaxing whenever any dark, rich color is used throughout a room. Your eye is not jumping from dark walls to light trim, and you sink into the color just as you'd sink into a comfortable sofa. It's almost as if you're swimming in it. And it opens up the space, because you can't see where the boundaries are."
EDDIE LEE

VALSPAR | SIGNATURE PURPLE ROYALTY 4009-10

"Imagine sitting back in a wicker chair on a veranda, sipping a martini, and reading F. Scott Fitzgerald. This lightest of greens has the dappled, fading light of a summer afternoon. It allows you to be quiet. It doesn't shout; it's still."

WHITNEY STEWART

C2 PAINT | LUXE SEEDLING C2-188

"Nothing is more soothing in a bedroom than this celestial blue. Pretty and fresh, it looks beautiful paired with virtually any color. I would put soft floral prints by Robert Kime or Bennison on the furniture. The room would feel like a garden, with the walls becoming the sky."

ALLISON CACCOMA

BENJAMIN MOORE | REGAL HARBOR HAZE 2136-60

"This cloudy shade of blue with gray undertones reminds me of the quietness of a rainy day, when you can just curl up in bed and relax. It would turn any room into a refuge. Combine it with more intense shades of gray and blue if you want more impact. A salmon or a deep sage would also look stunning against it."

PAUL CORRIE

BENJAMIN MOORE | REGAL SELECT BLUE LACE 1625

"I always wanted a lilac bedroom and went through a lot of shades before I found this one. The gray in it adds sophistication and takes it to a quiet, dreamy place. For accent colors, I chose earthy browns and creams, which have a serene effect and bring out the purple. If you pair it with brighter colors, it can get too juvenile and sweet."

RINAT LAVI

BENJAMIN MOORE | REGAL SELECT WINTER GRAY 2117-60

"I used this pink in my first studio apartment in New York. There was something about the combination of this color and the afternoon light pouring through the floor-to-ceiling windows that was so calming. You might think a pink apartment would scream 'girly girl,' but the gray undertones make it more sophisticated and grown-up."

ASHLEY WHITTAKER

FARROW & BALL | ESTATE EGGSHELL PINK GROUND 202

"I think it's the subtlety of this color that draws you in. It's the silvery gray-green of a eucalyptus leaf, with a soft, foggy quality that envelops you. It would be elegant in a dining room with dark woods and a rock-crystal chandelier, or calming in a master bath with Carrara marble. Gray veining would pick up the gray undertones."

LISA MCDENNON

SHERWIN-WILLIAMS |
HARMONY CONSERVATIVE GRAY SW 6183

"This is warm and inviting. It reminds me of the glow of the sun. When I look at it, I feel as if I'm on an island in the Caribbean, which is a retreat for me and where I find most of my inspiration. I'd layer it with natural linens and white trim."

ELSA SOYARS

BENJAMIN MOORE | REGAL CORAL GABLES 2010-40

"Grays are my new favorite neutral, and this one is wonderfully warm, with an organic feel. It can be casual and comforting or quietly elegant. I've used it in a dining room to create a sophisticated backdrop, but it could also be very relaxing in a bedroom. I like a satin finish for a richer look with greater durability."

ANN WISNIEWSKI

**SHERWIN-WILLIAMS |
EMERALD FAWN BRINDLE SW 7640**

"Everyone—men and women alike—loves this color. It's a pale blue with a lot of green in it, and it's a little dirty, which makes it more complex than the typical pastel. I've used it everywhere, from kitchens to bedrooms. I even painted my office in it. People walk in and say, 'This is how I want my house to feel.'"

CATHY KINCAID

FARROW & BALL | ESTATE EMULSION PALE POWDER 204

"Aqua reminds me of the carefree spirit of summer. This particular shade has more of a green cast, and that transports me to remote tropical beaches shaded by palm trees and lapped by waves— a perfect image for a bathroom. What's better than lying in the tub and being embraced by a color that captures that tranquillity?"

KERRY JOYCE

BENJAMIN MOORE | NATURA ST. JOHN'S BAY 584

"After a long day in New York City, I really want to go into a cocoon. And this deep, dark eggplant would completely envelop you. It conjures up Europe and the past but has a crispness that's contemporary too. I'd use it in a library, with an extra-deep leather sofa, old patinated brass, and a lime-green cashmere throw to snuggle up in. Don't disturb me."

SARA STORY

FARROW & BALL | PELT 254

"This delicate blue is the color of a husky's eyes, with just a touch of periwinkle in it to offset the sweetness. It's serene and soothing and especially gorgeous in a sitting room with crisp white tailored upholstery and Indian-print floral curtains."

SCHUYLER SAMPERTON

PRATT & LAMBERT | ASTRACHAN 27-30

Color Index

Shade by Shade

WHITE

SHERWIN-WILLIAMS
ALABASTER SW 7008

FARROW & BALL
ALL WHITE 2005

PRATT & LAMBERT
ANTIQUE WHITE 14-31

BENJAMIN MOORE
ATRIUM WHITE PM-13

FARROW & BALL
BLACKENED 2011

BENJAMIN MOORE
CHINA WHITE PM-20

WHITE *(continued)*

DONALD KAUFMAN COLOR
DKC-67

BENJAMIN MOORE
ELEPHANT TUSK OC-8

C2 PAINT
GOAT'S MILK BD1
2022-40

BENJAMIN MOORE
GRAYTINT 1611

FARROW & BALL
GREAT WHITE 2006

SHERWIN-WILLIAMS
GREEK VILLA 7551

MYLANDS
HOLLAND PARK NO. 5

BENJAMIN MOORE
HUNTINGTON WHITE
DC-02

C2 PAINT
MILK MOUSTACHE C2-692

FARROW & BALL
POINTING 2003

SHERWIN-WILLIAMS
RAMIE SW 6156

BEHR
SILKY WHITE

FARROW & BALL
STRONG WHITE 2001

BENJAMIN MOORE
SUPER WHITE

VALSPAR
SWISS COFFEE

VALSPAR
ULTRA WHITE 7006-24

BENJAMIN MOORE
WHITE DOVE OC-17

BEHR
WHITE TRUFFLE 720C-1

WHITE *(continued)*

FARROW & BALL
WIMBORNE WHITE 239

BENJAMIN MOORE
WINDS BREATH 981

PANTONE UNIVERSE
DELICACY 11-2409

BENJAMIN MOORE
MARBLE WHITE OC-34

BENJAMIN MOORE
SAN DIEGO CREAM 921

FARROW & BALL
WHITE TIE

TAN

BENJAMIN MOORE
COCOA SAND 1122

**DONALD KAUFMAN
COLOR**
DKC-09

FARROW & BALL
ENTRANCE HALL PINK 61

BEIGE

SHERWIN-WILLIAMS
CANVAS TAN SW 7531

BENJAMIN MOORE
BERKSHIRE BEIGE AC-2

BENJAMIN MOORE
HAZELWOOD 1005

BENJAMIN MOORE
HUSH AF-95

FARROW & BALL
DEAD FLAT MOUSE'S
BACK 40

FARROW & BALL
JOA'S WHITE 226

FARROW & BALL
STONY GROUND 211

SHERWIN-WILLIAMS
DOESKIN SW 6044

SHERWIN-WILLIAMS
NATURAL TAN SW 7567

GRAY

SHERWIN-WILLIAMS
ALOOF GRAY SW6197

SHERWIN-WILLIAMS
ANEW GRAY SW 7030

BENJAMIN MOORE
AURA CHELSEA GRAY
HC-168

BENJAMIN MOORE
AURA EARLY FROST
CSP-590

**DONALD KAUFMAN
COLOR**
BEACH GRASS GRAY

SHERWIN-WILLIAMS
BIG CHILL

BENJAMIN MOORE
BOOTHBAY GRAY HC-165

DUNN-EDWARDS PAINTS
CAVERNOUS DE6364

VALSPAR
CITY CHIC CI 51

BEHR
COCONUT ICE OR-W6

FARROW & BALL
CORNFORTH WHITE 228

BENJAMIN MOORE
DIOR GRAY 2133-40

PPG PITTSBURGH PAINTS
DOVER GRAY 1001-5

FARROW & BALL
DOWN PIPE 26

SHERWIN-WILLIAMS
EMERALD FAWN BRINDLE
SW 7640

FINE PAINTS OF EUROPE
G22730

BENJAMIN MOORE
GULL WING GRAY 2134-50

BENJAMIN MOORE
HIMALAYAN TREK 1542

GRAY *(continued)*

BENJAMIN MOORE
IRON MOUNTAIN
2134-30

BENJAMIN MOORE
KENDALL CHARCOAL
HC-166

BENJAMIN MOORE
LILY WHITE 2128-70

BENJAMIN MOORE
METALLIC SILVER
2132-60

BENJAMIN MOORE
METROPOLITAN AF-690

GLIDDEN
OLIVEWOOD 30YY 36/094

BENJAMIN MOORE
PAPER WHITE 1590

FARROW & BALL
PEIGNOIR 286

FARROW & BALL
PLUMMETT 272

FARROW & BALL
RAILINGS 31

SHERWIN-WILLIAMS
REPOSE GRAY SW 7015

SHERWIN-WILLIAMS
REQUISITE GRAY SW 7023

BENJAMIN MOORE
REVERE PEWTER HC-172

SHERWIN-WILLIAMS
SENSIBLE HUE SW 6198

BENJAMIN MOORE
SHORELINE 1471

FARROW & BALL
SKIMMING STONE 241

PORTOLA PAINTS & GLAZES
STONE 1

BENJAMIN MOORE
STONINGTON GRAY HC-170

GRAY *(continued)*

BENJAMIN MOORE
STORMY MONDAY
2112-50

BENJAMIN MOORE
TEMPTATION 1609

BENJAMIN MOORE
TWEED COAT CSP-85

BLACK

BENJAMIN MOORE
WICKHAM GRAY HC-171

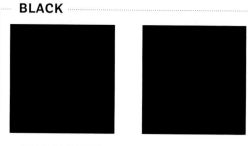

PRATT & LAMBERT
ANUBIS 32-17

BENJAMIN MOORE
BLACK 2132-10

CLARK+KENSINGTON
BLACK CHIFFON N-C15

BENJAMIN MOORE
BLACK HC-190

BEHR
BLACK SUEDE S-H-790

BENJAMIN MOORE
GRAY 2121-10

FARROW & BALL
OFF-BLACK 57

FARROW & BALL
PITCH BLACK 256

BROWN

VALSPAR
SIGNATURE TUXEDO TIE
AR2104

VALSPAR
SIGNATURE VERY BLACK
5011-2

PRATT & LAMBERT
ACCOLADE BLACK COFFEE
3-19

BENJAMIN MOORE
BARISTA AF-175

SHERWIN-WILLIAMS
BLACK BEAN SW 6006

SHERWIN-WILLIAMS
BLACK FOX SW 7020

BROWN *(continued)*

C2 PAINT
BUCKAROO C2-615

C2 PAINT
CATTAIL BD 48

BENJAMIN MOORE
CHOCOLATE CANDY
BROWN 2107-10

FINE PAINTS OF EUROPE
E25-30

FINE PAINTS OF EUROPE
E25-44

FARROW & BALL
MAHOGANY 36

SHERWIN-WILLIAMS
SABLE SW 6083

FARROW & BALL
TANNER'S BROWN 255

BENJAMIN MOORE
WHISPERING WOODS
1012

PURPLE

BENJAMIN MOORE
ANGELINA 1376

SHERWIN-WILLIAMS
AWESOME VIOLET SW
6815

FARROW & BALL
BRASSICA 271

BENJAMIN MOORE
CENTURY ACAI R8

PRATT & LAMBERT
CONFIDENTIAL 29-17

BENJAMIN MOORE
DARK LILAC 2070-30

SHERWIN-WILLIAMS
DAYDREAM SW 6541

SHERWIN-WILLIAMS
DEWBERRY SW 6552

**DONALD KAUFMAN
COLOR**
DKC-36

PURPLE *(continued)*

SHERWIN-WILLIAMS
ELATION SW 6827

SHERWIN-WILLIAMS
EMERALD RAISIN SW 7630

BENJAMIN MOORE
FREESIA 1432

FARROW & BALL
FULL GLOSS BRINJAL 222

FINE PAINTS OF EUROPE
G17140

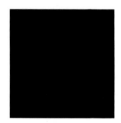

BENJAMIN MOORE
GALAXY 2117-20

BENJAMIN MOORE
GRAPPA 1393

FINE PAINTS OF EUROPE
H04320

PRATT & LAMBERT
HALF LIGHT 29-2

BENJAMIN MOORE
ICED LAVENDER 1410

BENJAMIN MOORE
INSPIRED AF-595

BENJAMIN MOORE
LAVENDER MIST 2070-60

BENJAMIN MOORE
NOSEGAY 1401

FINE PAINTS OF EUROPE
OPHELIA VIOLET 7172

FARROW & BALL
PELT 254

PRATT & LAMBERT
QUARTZ MOON 31-29

SHERWIN-WILLIAMS
QUEEN ANNE LILAC SW
0021

BENJAMIN MOORE
REGAL SELECT GRAPE
JUICE 2074-10

PURPLE *(continued)*

BENJAMIN MOORE
REGAL SELECT WINTER
GRAY 2117-60

BENJAMIN MOORE
SHADOW 2117-30

VALSPAR
SIGNATURE PURPLE
ROYALTY 4009-10

BENJAMIN MOORE
SPRING LILAC 1388

BENJAMIN MOORE
TWILIGHT MAGENTA
2074-30

DUNN-EDWARDS PAINTS
VIOLET CRUSH DE5946

PINK

BENJAMIN MOORE
VIOLET DUSK 1409

SHERWIN-WILLIAMS
WALLFLOWER SW 6281

SHERWIN-WILLIAMS
ANGELIC SW 6602

PRATT & LAMBERT
AZALEA 5-12

C2 PAINT
BELLE'S NOSE BD 50

BENJAMIN MOORE
BERMUDA PINK 016

FARROW & BALL
CALAMINE 230

FINE PAINTS OF EUROPE
CAMELLIA PINK

BENJAMIN MOORE
CORAL GLOW 026

PRATT & LAMBERT
COY PINK 3-28

BENJAMIN MOORE
CRUSHED VELVET
2076-10

VALSPAR
DANCE OF THE
GODDESSES 23-1A

PINK *(continued)*

SHERWIN-WILLIAMS
DRAGON FRUIT SW 6855

FINE PAINTS OF EUROPE
E3-1

FINE PAINTS OF EUROPE
E3-26

PRATT & LAMBERT
ENCHANTRESS 3-10

SHERWIN-WILLIAMS
EXUBERANT PINK SW
6840

BENJAMIN MOORE
FAIREST PINK 2092-70

BENJAMIN MOORE
FOGGY MORNING 2106-
70

FARROW & BALL
FOWLER PINK 39

GLIDDEN
FRESH PINK LEMONADE
GLR17

BENJAMIN MOORE
FRUIT SHAKE 2088-60

KT.COLOR
HOT MAGENTA 06.001

SHERWIN-WILLIAMS
INNOCENCE SW 6302

BENJAMIN MOORE
ITALIANO ROSE 2087-30

SHERWIN-WILLIAMS
JAZZ AGE CORAL SW 0058

BENJAMIN MOORE
MILK SHAKE 1165

FARROW & BALL
NANCY'S BLUSHES 278

BENJAMIN MOORE
OPAL OC-73

**PORTOLA PAINTS &
GLAZES**
PARIS PINK PC 106

PINK *(continued)*

SHERWIN-WILLIAMS
PARTYTIME SW 6849

BENJAMIN MOORE
PEONY 2079-30

C2 PAINT
PILLOW TALK C2-514

FARROW & BALL
PINK GROUND 202

BENJAMIN MOORE
PINK LACE 2081-60

BENJAMIN MOORE
PINK SWIRL 2171-70

BENJAMIN MOORE
QUEEN ANNE PINK HC-60

BENJAMIN MOORE
REGAL CORAL GABLES
2010-40

BENJAMIN MOORE
REGAL SELECT OLD
WORLD 2011-40

BENJAMIN MOORE
SALMON PEACH 2013-50

FARROW & BALL
SETTING PLASTER 231

PORTOLA PAINTS & GLAZES
STARMAN

PRATT & LAMBERT
SWEET MIST 3-30

BENJAMIN MOORE
TICKLED PINK 2002-50

BENJAMIN MOORE
WARM BLUSH 892

RED

FINE PAINTS OF EUROPE
WINDSOR PINK

SHERWIN-WILLIAMS
BOLERO SW 7600

FARROW & BALL
BOOK ROOM RED 50

RED *(continued)*

**DONALD KAUFMAN
COLOR**
DKC-17

FINE PAINTS OF EUROPE
E10-59

SHERWIN-WILLIAMS
EMERALD RED TOMATO
SW 6607

FARROW & BALL
ETRUSCAN RED 56

BENJAMIN MOORE
HABANERO PEPPER 1306

BENJAMIN MOORE
HERITAGE RED PM-18

FARROW & BALL
INCARNADINE 248

FARROW & BALL
PICTURE GALLERY RED 42

FINE PAINTS OF EUROPE
POST OFFICE RED BS
0006

BENJAMIN MOORE
RAVISHING RED 2008-10

FARROW & BALL
RECTORY RED 217

GLIDDEN
RED DELICIOUS GLR30

FARROW & BALL
RED EARTH 64

BEHR
RODEO RED 200D-7

FINE PAINTS OF EUROPE
TULIP RED 1001

ORANGE

C2 PAINT
TURKISH MARKET C2-571

BENJAMIN MOORE
UMBRIA RED 1316

BENJAMIN MOORE
BURNT CARAMEL 2167-10

ORANGE *(continued)*

BENJAMIN MOORE
CALYPSO ORANGE
2015-30

SHERWIN-WILLIAMS
CARNIVAL SW 6892

BENJAMIN MOORE
ELECTRIC ORANGE
2015-10

BENJAMIN MOORE
MELON POPSICLE
2016-50

SHERWIN-WILLIAMS
OBSTINATE ORANGE SW

DUNN-EDWARDS PAINTS
ORANGE DAYLILY DE5145

BENJAMIN MOORE
REGAL SELECT ORANGE
PARROT 2169-20

SHERWIN-WILLIAMS
SUNSET SW 6626

SHERWIN-WILLIAMS
YAM SW 6643

YELLOW

BENJAMIN MOORE
AURA 169

BENJAMIN MOORE
BANANA YELLOW 2022-40

FARROW & BALL
CITRON 74

BENJAMIN MOORE
CORN SILK CC-218

SHERWIN-WILLIAMS
DAISY SW 6910

DONALD KAUFMAN COLOR
DKC-42

SHERWIN-WILLIAMS
GOLDFINCH SW 6905

FINE PAINTS OF EUROPE
H01610

FINE PAINTS OF EUROPE
IVORY PALM 6012P

YELLOW *(continued)*

PPG PITTSBURGH PAINTS
LOTUS FLOWER 1206-1

PORTOLA PAINTS & GLAZES
LOTUS PC195

PRATT & LAMBERT
MILK WHITE 15-32

GLIDDEN
PREMIUM COLLECTION
CRISP GINGER ALE GLY24

PRATT & LAMBERT
SHANTUNG 11-2

VALSPAR
SOFT DUCKLING 3001-2A

GREEN

GLIDDEN
SPICY BANANA PEPPER
50YY 60/538

BENJAMIN MOORE
ADVANCE KELLY GREEN
2037-30

FARROW & BALL
ARSENIC 214

BENJAMIN MOORE
ARTICHOKE HEARTS 382

BENJAMIN MOORE
PALE AVOCADO 2146-40

BENJAMIN MOORE
BABY FERN 2029-20

SHERWIN-WILLIAMS
BONSAI TINT SW 6436

FARROW & BALL
CARD ROOM GREEN 79

FARROW & BALL
CHAPPELL GREEN 83

C2 PAINT
CHARGREEN C2-694

FULL SPECTRUM PAINTS
CHARTREUSE

GLIDDEN
DEEP FOREST PINE 30GG
09/106

GREEN *(continued)*

**DONALD KAUFMAN
COLOR**
DKC-102

**DONALD KAUFMAN
COLOR**
DKC-63

BENJAMIN MOORE
DRAGONWELL CSP-930

FINE PAINTS OF EUROPE
E25-05

FINE PAINTS OF EUROPE
E13-15

FINE PAINTS OF EUROPE
E7-53

SHERWIN-WILLIAMS
ESPALIER SW 6734

BENJAMIN MOORE
ESSEX GREEN RME-43

FARROW & BALL
ESTATE EGGSHELL
CHURLISH GREEN 251

FARROW & BALL
ESTATE EGGSHELL
LICHEN 19

BENJAMIN MOORE
EVE GREEN 2024-20

**PORTOLA PAINTS &
GLAZES**
FOUNTAIN STONE PC306

SHERWIN-WILLIAMS
GREAT GREEN SW 6430

GLIDDEN
GREEN GRAPE 88YY
66/447

SHERWIN-WILLIAMS
GREENS SW 6748

FINE PAINTS OF EUROPE
H03010

BENJAMIN MOORE
HANCOCK GREEN HC-117

SHERWIN-WILLIAMS
HIGH STRUNG SW 6705

GREEN *(continued)*

**PORTOLA PAINTS &
GLAZES**
HYDE PARK 107

BENJAMIN MOORE
ITALIAN ICE GREEN
2035-70

SHERWIN-WILLIAMS
LIME GRANITA SW 6715

BENJAMIN MOORE
LIME RICKY 393

FINE PAINTS OF EUROPE
LINDEN BS12E53

SHERWIN-WILLIAMS
LOUNGE GREEN SW 6444

C2 PAINT
LUXE SEEDLING C2-188

**SYDNEY HARBOUR
PAINTS**
MANUKA

BENJAMIN MOORE
MARGARITA 2026-20

PRATT & LAMBERT
MIDDLESTONE 12-22

BENJAMIN MOORE
MISTED FERN 482

FARROW & BALL
OLIVE 13

SHERWIN-WILLIAMS
RELENTLESS OLIVE SW
6425

BENJAMIN MOORE
SAVANNAH MOSS 385

SHERWIN-WILLIAMS
SECRET GARDEN SW 6181

FINE PAINTS OF EUROPE
SMALL DINING ROOM
GREEN MV3

BENJAMIN MOORE
SPRING BUD 520

BENJAMIN MOORE
ST. ELMO'S FIRE 362

GREEN *(continued)*

BENJAMIN MOORE
STOLEN MOMENTS 477

FARROW & BALL
STONE WHITE 11

FARROW & BALL
STUDIO GREEN 93

BENJAMIN MOORE
THORNTON SAGE 464

BENJAMIN MOORE
TUSCANY GREEN 2140-20

FARROW & BALL
VERT DE TERRE 234

GREEN-GRAY

FINE PAINTS OF EUROPE
WILLOW BS12B17

FARROW & BALL
CARRIAGE GREEN 94

PORTOLA PAINTS & GLAZES
FALLING TIDE 087

FARROW & BALL
GREEN SMOKE 47

SHERWIN-WILLIAMS
HARMONY CONSERVATIVE
GRAY SW 6183

GLIDDEN
KHAKI GREEN 60YY
33/130

BLUE

BENJAMIN MOORE
NANTUCKET GRAY HC-111

VALSPAR
SIGNATURE SPARKLING
SAGE 5005-3B

PRATT & LAMBERT
ACCOLADE SMOKE RING
26-1

BENJAMIN MOORE
ADVANCE TROPICANA
CABANA 2048-50

BENJAMIN MOORE
ANTIGUAN SKY 2040-60

C2 PAINT
ARGYLE C2-751

BLUE *(continued)*

PRATT & LAMBERT
ASTRACHAN 27-30

BENJAMIN MOORE
ATHENS BLUE 797

BENJAMIN MOORE
AURA HOW BLUE AM I?
752

BENJAMIN MOORE
AURA KENTUCKY HAZE
AC-16

BENJAMIN MOORE
AURA SAILOR'S SEA BLUE
2063-40

BENJAMIN MOORE
AURA SANTA MONICA
BLUE 776

FARROW & BALL
BALLROOM BLUE 24

FARROW & BALL
BLACK BLUE 95

BENJAMIN MOORE
BLUE BONNET 2050-70

SHERWIN-WILLIAMS
BLUE CRUISE SW 7606

BENJAMIN MOORE
BLUE HAZE 1667

FARROW & BALL
BORROWED LIGHT 235

BENJAMIN MOORE
CARIBBEAN AZURE
2059-20

SHERWIN-WILLIAMS
DEBONAIR SW 9139

PRATT & LAMBERT
DECEMBER EVE 23-02

BENJAMIN MOORE
DEEP ROYAL 2061-10

FINE PAINTS OF EUROPE
DEEP SAXE BLUE BS113

SHERWIN-WILLIAMS
DIGNITY BLUE SW 6804

BLUE *(continued)*

DUNN-EDWARDS PAINTS
DIVE IN DE5895

FARROW & BALL
DRAWING ROOM BLUE
253

**RESTORATION
HARDWARE**
DUSK

FINE PAINTS OF EUROPE
E25-63

SHERWIN-WILLIAMS
EMERALD MAJOR BLUE
6795

BENJAMIN MOORE
EVENING BLUE 2066-20

DUNN-EDWARDS PAINTS
EVEREST DRENCHED RAIN
DE5883

BENJAMIN MOORE
FADED DENIM 795

BENJAMIN MOORE
GOSSAMER BLUE 2123-40

SHERWIN-WILLIAMS
GULFSTREAM SW6766

FARROW & BALL
HAGUE BLUE 30

BENJAMIN MOORE
HALE NAVY HC-154

SHERWIN-WILLIAMS
HONEST BLUE SW 6520

FARROW & BALL
INCHYRA BLUE 289

FARROW & BALL
LULWORTH BLUE 89

VALSPAR
LYNDHURST CELESTIAL
BLUE 5003-9C

PRATT & LAMBERT
MIDSUMMER GALE 26-17

BEHR
MISTY MORN PPU12-10

BLUE *(continued)*

PRATT & LAMBERT
NANKING BLUE 23-10

SHERWIN-WILLIAMS
NAVAL SW 6244

FINE PAINTS OF EUROPE
NAVY BLUE 1798

FINE PAINTS OF EUROPE
NCS S 2020-R90B

BENJAMIN MOORE
NEW YORK STATE OF
MIND 805

BENJAMIN MOORE
NEWBURYPORT BLUE
HC-155

BENJAMIN MOORE
NORTH SEA CC-932

SHERWIN-WILLIAMS
NORTH STAR SW 6246

BENJAMIN MOORE
NOVA SCOTIA BLUE 796

BENJAMIN MOORE
OCEAN SPRAY 2047-60

BENJAMIN MOORE
OLD GLORY 811

BENJAMIN MOORE
PALE SMOKE 1584

FARROW & BALL
PAVILION BLUE 252

FINE PAINTS OF EUROPE
POTOMAC BLUE MV23

GLIDDEN
PREMIUM CARIBBEAN SEA
GLB02

BENJAMIN MOORE
REGAL HARBOR HAZE
2136-60

BENJAMIN MOORE
REGAL SELECT BLUE VEIL
875

BENJAMIN MOORE
REGAL SELECT POLO
BLUE 2062-10

BLUE *(continued)*

FINE PAINTS OF EUROPE
S 3040-B10G

FARROW & BALL
SKYLIGHT 205

SHERWIN-WILLIAMS
SLEEPY BLUE SW 6225

DUNN-EDWARDS PAINTS
SPEARMINT DE5729

FARROW & BALL
STIFFKEY BLUE 281

PANTONE UNIVERSE
STILLWATER 16-4610

SHERWIN-WILLIAMS
TEMPE STAR SW 6229

BEHR
TIBETAN TURQUOISE
MQ4-53

BENJAMIN MOORE
ULTRA SPEC 500 OASIS
BLUE 2049-40

BENJAMIN MOORE
UN-TEAL WE MEET AGAIN
739

BENJAMIN MOORE
VAN COURTLAND BLUE
HC-145

FINE PAINTS OF EUROPE
WC-77

FINE PAINTS OF EUROPE
WC-86

FINE PAINTS OF EUROPE
WC-90

PRATT & LAMBERT
WHITE SMOKE 26-2

BLUE-GRAY

PPG PITTSBURGH PAINTS
BLUE DOLPHIN 1041-4

FARROW & BALL
BLUE GRAY 91

BENJAMIN MOORE
ICED CUBE SILVER
2121-50

BLUE-GRAY *(continued)*

C2 PAINT
KIND OF BLUE C2-772

RESTORATION HARDWARE
LIGHT SILVER SAGE

SHERWIN-WILLIAMS
MISTY SW 6232

FARROW & BALL
MODERN EMULSION
LIGHT BLUE 22

PANTONE UNIVERSE
MONUMENT 17-4405

FARROW & BALL
OVAL ROOM BLUE 85

C2 PAINT
OVERCAST C2-738

FARROW & BALL
PARMA GRAY 27

BENJAMIN MOORE
REGAL SELECT BLUE
LACE 1625

**PORTOLA PAINTS &
GLAZES**
SEAL 086

SHERWIN-WILLIAMS
ST. BART'S SW 7614

SHERWIN-WILLIAMS
STILL WATER SW 6223

BLUE-GREEN

BENJAMIN MOORE
AZURE WATER 677

MARTIN SENOUR PAINTS
BLEACHED PILING 1125-A

FARROW & BALL
DIX BLUE 82

FARROW & BALL
GREEN BLUE 84

BENJAMIN MOORE
GULF STREAM 670

BENJAMIN MOORE
HEALING ALOE 1562

BLUE-GREEN *(continued)*

GLIDDEN
ICY TEAL 50GG 55/049

BENJAMIN MOORE
MEXICALI TURQUOISE
662

VALSPAR
MYSTIC SEA 5007-7A

BENJAMIN MOORE
NATURA ST. JOHN'S BAY
584

FARROW & BALL
PALE POWDER 204

BENJAMIN MOORE
PALLADIAN BLUE HC-144

C2 PAINT
POND SHIMMER BD-24

VALSPAR
SIGNATURE TURQUOISE
TINT 5006-10B

BENJAMIN MOORE
ST. LUCIA TEAL 683

BENJAMIN MOORE
TEAL OCEAN 2049-30

FARROW & BALL
TERESA'S GREEN 236

SHERWIN-WILLIAMS
TIDEWATER SW 6477

BENJAMIN MOORE
TROPICAL TURQUOISE
2052-30

BENJAMIN MOORE
WYTHE BLUE HC-143

Photography Credits

© Edward Addeo: 107

© Lucas Allen: 36

© Patrick Argast: 92

© Michel Arnaud: 167

© Gordon Beall: 137, 199

© Chad Chenier: 184

© Patrick Cline: 220

© John Cole: 119

© Michael Croteau: 28

© Roger Davies: 182

© Erica George Dines: 26

© Miki Duisterhof: 214

© David Duncan: 139

© Phillip Ennis: 223

© Pieter Estersohn: 44, 58, 200

© Miguel Flores-Vianna: 52

© Emily Followill: 2, 116

© Gianni Franchelucci: 81

© Freer Gallery of Art and Arthur M. Sackler Gallery, Smithsonian Institution, Washington, D.C.: Gift of Charles Lang Freer, F1904.61: 123

Getty Images: © Frank Krahmer: 142

© Tria Giovan: 20, 68, 128, 164

© Susan Gilmore: 10

© John Healey: 16

© Francesco Lagnese: 74, 147

© Neil Landino: 25

© Manolo Langis: 150

© Michael J. Lee: 83, 196

© Thomas Loof: 40

© Janet Mesic Mackie: 154

© Read McKendree/courtesy of Philip Gorrivan: 113

© Maura McEvoy: 67, 108

© Joshua McHugh: 86

© courtesy of Mimi McMakin of Kemble Interiors: 168

© Dana Meilijson: 6, 217

© Karyn Millet: 56

© Derry Moore: 98, 111

© Michael Mundy: 205

© Nancy Nolan: 8, 50, 64, 172

© David Oliver: 203

© Eric Piasecki: 135

© Aubrie Pick: 208

© Paul Raeside: 177

Lara Robby/Studio D: 30

© Lisa Romerein: 148, 172, 178

© Stephanie Sabbe: 77

© Durston Saylor: 226

© Lance Selgo: 187

© Alan Shortall: 4, 48

© Tim Street-Porter: 73

© Peter Turman: 60

© Jonny Valiant: 100

© Cynthia Van Elk: 47

© William Waldron: 160

© Bjorn Wallander: 190

© Christina Wedge: 89

© Paul Whicheloe: 94

All paint swatches by Stuart Tyson/Studio D

Index

HEARSTBOOKS

An Imprint of Sterling Publishing Co., Inc.
1166 Avenue of the Americas
New York, NY 10036

ISBN 978-1-61837-258-1

Distributed in Canada by Sterling Publishing
c/o Canadian Manda Group, 664 Annette Street
Toronto, Ontario M6S 2C8, Canada
Distributed in the United Kingdom by GMC Distribution Services
Castle Place, 166 High Street, Lewes, East Sussex BN7 1XU, England
Distributed in Australia by NewSouth Books
45 Beach Street, Coogee, NSW 2034, Australia

For information about custom editions, special sales, and premium and corporate purchases, please contact Sterling Special Sales at 800-805-5489 or specialsales@sterlingpublishing.com.

Manufactured in China

2 4 6 8 10 9 7 5 3 1

sterlingpublishing.com
housebeautiful.com

Cover design by Elizabeth Mihaltse Lindy
Interior design by Nancy Singer
Photography credits on page 272